D1341701

'LET HIM HAVE IT, CHRIS'

'LET HIM HAVE IT, CHRIS'

The murder of Derek Bentley

M. J. TROW

Constable · London

First published in Great Britain 1990
by Constable and Company Limited
3 The Lanchesters
162 Fulham Palace Road
London W6 9ER
Copyright © 1990 by M. J. Trow
ISBN 0 09 469700 0
Set in Linotron Sabon 11pt by
Rowland Phototypesetting Limited
Bury St Edmunds, Suffolk
Printed in Great Britain by
St Edmundsbury Press Limited
Bury St Edmunds, Suffolk

A CIP catalogue record for this book
is available from the British Library

'Those who still "look back in anger" upon the miscarriage of justice should not cease from mental fight, until such happenings in England are impossible.'

C. G. L. Du Cann

Miscarriages of Justice (1960)

CONTENTS

ILLUSTRATIONS

ACKNOWLEDGEMENTS

I came upon the Craig and Bentley case by accident. In the summer of 1988 my wife learned to drive on a 'crash' course lasting five days. On the first day, she was back after an hour with her instructor who had heard I was a writer and said, 'Have I got a book for you!'

I thought he was pulling my leg. 'Ah,' I said, '"Death of a Driving Instructor"?'

But it emerged that he had something much more serious in mind. His name was Ray Pain and his father's previously unpublished testimony is the cornerstone of this book. So I would like to say thank you first of all to Ray and above all to Claude Pain. But the book would have been impossible without the co-operation and inspiration of a lot of others and I would like to take this opportunity to thank them. To Ludovic Kennedy, long a campaigner for the truth, for writing the Foreword; to my agent Andrew Lownie who has become, like many of us, caught up in the 'quiet crusade'; to Ben Glazebrook, my publisher, for putting me into print and to June Bassett for her excellent copy-editing; to Iris Bentley and her daughter Maria for whom the fight goes on; to various authors listed in the bibliography for allowing me to quote from their works; to April Goodey of Scotland Yard's Press office; to Mrs Beecher-Brigden for her reminiscences of the night in question.

And most of all to my wife, who not only talked me through the Craig and Bentley case twist by twist, but sat at the word processor night after night crying for Derek Bentley.

M. J. Trow
October 1989

FOREWORD

by Ludovic Kennedy

It is my belief that murder cases which continue to be discussed and argued about years and often decades after sentences have been handed down and appeals dismissed, are those in which justice, in some degree, has miscarried; cases like those of Evans and Christie. James Hanratty, Patrick Meehan, the Luton Post Office murder. The murder of Maxwell Confait, the Carl Bridgewater case, the murder of PC Blakelock, the cases of the Guildford Four and the Birmingham Six. In some of the cases, like those of Evans and Meehan and the Guildford Four, the miscarriage has been admitted and restitution of a kind made. In others, like those of James Hanratty, the two convicted in the Luton case and the Birmingham Six, the original verdicts have been allowed to stand, but despite dismissals by the Appeal Court they cannot be said to be safe and satisfactory.

It is Mr Trow's belief that another of the more notorious of post-war cases, that of the conviction of the sixteen-year-old Christopher Craig and of the nineteen-year-old Derek Bentley for what has become known as the Croydon roof-top murder falls into the latter category. The bare facts of the case were that on a November night in 1952 Craig, armed with a loaded revolver and knuckle duster, and Bentley, carrying a knife, were spotted breaking in to Messrs Parker and Barlow's confectionery warehouse in Croydon. The police arrived, and there was a confrontation on the rooftop. Bentley was taken into custody fairly early on, but Craig fired his revolver several times, wounding one officer, Detective Constable Fairfax, slightly, and killing another, Police Constable Miles, stone dead. Five weeks later the pair were tried for murder before the Lord Chief Justice, Lord Goddard, at the Old Bailey. Both were found guilty. Craig, being too young to be hanged, was ordered to be detained during Her Majesty's pleasure. Bentley, whom the jury recommended to mercy, was sentenced to death.

At the trial, Lord Goddard explained to the jury that when two or more people are engaged jointly on a felonious enterprise and murder results, each in law, and irrespective of who caused the murder, is as responsible as the other. That being so, the jury had no choice but to bring in a double verdict of guilty; and Goddard himself had no choice but to impose the mandatory sentence of death.

Yet there were few people in Britain at that time who thought that Bentley would be called on to pay the full penalty. Whatever the law might say on the matter, it seemed contrary to natural justice that he who had fired the fatal shot should only be required to go to prison for a few years while his accomplice, who had been in police custody at the time of the shooting, should be considered so irredeemable as to be hanged. Furthermore Bentley had had a wretched childhood, first having had to be dug out of his home after it had been destroyed by the Luftwaffe; then having been concussed by a fall which led to epileptic fits, as a result of which he could neither read nor write and had an IQ of 66 and mental powers of a 4½ year old.

But the Home Secretary of the time, a lawyer by the name of Maxwell Fyfe (later Lord Kilmuir) took a different view: the murder of a police officer in the execution of his duty was the most serious of crimes: they and the public must be protected from those who might have similar ideas of lawlessness; and two days before Bentley was due to hang, and despite petitions to the Home Secretary, the Prime Minister and the Queen, despite protests in Parliament and the newspapers and marches through the streets, Maxwell Fyfe announced that the law must take its course.

Both my wife and myself were profoundly shocked by Maxwell Fyfe's decision, and on the eve of Bentley's execution sent him, as I found later, many others did, a telegram urging him to stay his hand – a fruitless gesture yet one which we felt we had to make. That night and again in the early morning, when a large crowd began assembling outside the gates of Wandsworth prison, our thoughts were with the wretched youth in his cell, waiting for the hangman to come. Indeed, long after Bentley's corpse had been cut down and buried in quicklime in the prison precincts, I could not rid my mind of what we, as a society, had done to him; and later that year I wrote a play called *Murder Story*, based on the case, and in which a youth similar to Bentley suffers a similar fate. It was first put on by the Aldershot

Repertory Company and later transferred to the West End. It was well received by the critics, but because of the subject-matter, did not run for more than a couple of months: however it was adapted for television, and for a couple of years afterwards was performed by a number of repertory and amateur companies. It became, though I did not realize it at the time, the genesis of all my subsequent works on miscarriages of criminal justice.

Apart from *Murder Story*, much else has been written in the way of articles, books, radio and television documentaries on the subject of the Croydon case. Most have been inspired, as my play was, by the idea of the denial of natural justice. I guess that this has been the mainspring of Mr Trow's book too, though as a result of his painstaking researches he has been able to go further than anyone before him. For he is saying not only that Bentley's death was a denial of natural justice but that *there was a clear miscarriage of justice on the facts too*.

What is Mr Trow's evidence for this? It comes from an eighty-year-old retired police officer by the name of Claude Pain now living in retirement and who told Mr Trow that his conscience had been troubling him that he had not spoken up earlier. For Claude Pain was on the warehouse rooftop with all the other officers. Yet his name does not figure in any of their depositions and he was not called as a witness at the trial. Why? Because his account of what he heard them say and not say differed fundamentally from theirs.

I do not think there can be much dispute that the final nail in Bentley's coffin, the one piece of evidence that persuaded Maxwell Fyfe not to grant him a reprieve was what was said by three of the police officers confronting Craig on the roof. This was that after he had been apprehended by the police, Bentley shouted to Craig, 'Let him have it, Chris', whereupon Craig opened fire.

Both Bentley and Craig denied that Bentley ever said this, but some writers, considering the import of the words, have suggested that Bentley's cry was not a request to Craig to open fire, but rather a plea to hand the gun over. But Mr Trow will have none of this because Claude Pain will have none of it and – more important – would have none of it when it came to writing his deposition in November 1952 of what he saw and heard on the roof: 'I did not write it down because I did not hear it. *I did not write it down because it was not said.*'

There are other reasons for supposing that it was not said. Firstly, it would have been entirely out of character for Bentley to have expressed himself so forcibly. He was of a passive nature, easily led, as the dominant partner in their relationship, Christopher Craig, knew only too well. (It was the 16-year-old Craig who had persuaded the 19-year-old Bentley to join him on the enterprise, not the other way round). Secondly, Bentley never called Craig 'Chris', but 'kid' or 'kiddo'. Thirdly, while there was every reason for Bentley to deny having said it, there was no reason for Craig to deny it if true: indeed if Bentley *had* said it, Craig might have claimed as part of his defence that it was this that had triggered him into firing the fatal shot. And Craig in evidence was quite emphatic that Bentley had not said it:

'Are you saying', prosecuting counsel asked him, 'that you did not hear that?' ['Let him have it, Chris']

'Bentley did not say it, sir.'

'Three officers heard it in the darkness from different points of the compass. Are you saying he did not say it?'

'I am saying I did not hear it,' Craig replied, 'and if they heard it, they have better ears than mine.'

So if Craig and Bentley and Claude Pain are all agreed that Bentley never said, 'Let him have it, Chris', it is very possible that he did not say it. Nevertheless, referring to the bravery of the three officers in his charge to the jury, Lord Goddard added, 'Are you going to say they are conspicuous liars?', and the barrister and legal chronicler, H. Montgomery Hyde, said that it would be difficult if not impossible for a jury 'to believe that responsible police officers should have deliberately fabricated their evidence in a capital trial'.

They did not believe it; and yet, as Mr Trow makes clear, there is now every reason why we should believe it. From the police's view, one of their number had been cold-bloodedly killed by one of the two defendants. Understandably they wanted a life for a life; and if it could not be extracted from the defendant who had fired the shot because he was too young to hang, then his co-defendant and partner in crime would do just as well. To give credibility to this theory, one does not have to presuppose the three officers jointly and deliberately agreeing to put into Bentley's mouth words he did not utter. It does not happen like that. It would only require one of the officers, for such is the power of self-delusion, to voice an opinion that Bentley had shouted some encouragement to Craig for the others gladly to seize on it and then for all to try to 'remember' just what it was that Craig had said. The words 'Let him have it, Chris!' would have evolved gradually, and by the time they had been agreed on, all three officers would have completely convinced themselves that that is what they had heard Bentley shout.

But Claude Pain could not be of their number. He had written a deposition in which he had made no mention of Bentley shouting anything, and one would like to think that, asked by his colleagues to join their club, he refused to compromise his integrity. Yet he, no less than they, had felt the death of PC Miles keenly; and police solidarity being necessary not only for their morale but their survival, there could be no question of him disassociating himself from their evidence. So, although a witness on the roof along with the rest of them, he does not figure anywhere in his colleagues' presentation of their case: indeed they denied on oath that there was any other officer on the roof besides themselves. He was not cited as a witness; and soon after his notebook and his deposition 'disappeared'.

I imagine that most readers will be happy to accept Mr Trow's reassessment of the extent of Bentley's culpability in the light of the new evidence from Mr Pain; though I will be surprised if they are as ready as he is to exculpate Craig on the grounds that he was firing to frighten the police and not with the intention of killing them. But what I think all readers will endorse is Mr Trow's resentment at being denied access to the case papers being held under lock and key at the Public Record Office, and a study of which would surely clear up most of its mysteries and ambiguities. When he asked if he could have a peep at them, he was told that they were not to be released for public view until the year 2047, by which time, he says, he will be 98. 'Can the British judicial system', he asks, 'really be so frail that it cannot rattle its skeletons in the open and not in some cupboard at Kew?' But it is less the British judicial system that is at fault here than its political masters, for whom obsessive secrecy, the stifling rather than the freeing of information, seems almost to have become a way of life.

—— 1 ——
'NOW, THE STORY IS THIS . . .'

The doorbell rang for the second time that evening, momentarily diverting the boys from the television, blinking from its nine inches of black and white across the living-room. William Bentley bounced to his feet and was in the hall. If it was that Craig kid again, he'd have a go at him. For all his big talk of jobs and gangs, he was only a little bastard of sixteen. Not that William Bentley ever swore in front of his family or in his own house. But Craig seemed to bring out the worst in everybody.

But Lilian, his wife, had reached the door ahead of him. William Bentley couldn't see the figure beyond her, but the voice sounded polite, educated.

'That's not Craig,' he said, half to himself.

His son Derek agreed, shaking his head. He was sitting watching the television, still wearing his best clothes. He had come home early from the pictures with one of his headaches. The headaches which had got worse again recently. The headaches which were not likely to go away. Not even the charms of Betty Grable on the big screen prevented its onset. The picture had bobbed and wobbled in front of him. He had pushed his way to the aisle in the darkness and muttered to the usherette that he was going home. She was Iris, his big sister. She understood.

Lilian Bentley stood talking on the doorstep for a good three minutes. Then she came back –

'It's a boy named Norman Parsley,' she told the family. 'He wants Derek to go out for a walk with him. Who is he, Derek? I've never heard you mention his name.'

Derek Bentley breathed a sigh of relief. It wasn't Craig. The phenobarbs he'd taken were beginning to work. He felt easier, slower perhaps, as though in a thick haze. But the sickening throbbing in his

*head was going away. His mum had seen Craig off earlier in the day.
Now he felt safe. It was all right. It wasn't Craig. It was Norman
Parsley.*

'He's all right, Mum. He's a good bloke.'

*Lilian Bentley looked at her husband, sensing his doubt, his
apprehension. 'He's so nice-looking, Will,' she said. 'So well-
mannered. Seems like a college boy to me.'*

'He is, Mum,' Derek assured them both, 'he's an educated bloke.'

*An educated bloke. What was an educated bloke doing, hanging
around Derek? William was educated too, after his own fashion. He'd
trained at Guy's Hospital, had diplomas in midwifery and first aid.
There had been talk, years ago, of a scholarship to Oxford. But it
wasn't superior education that faced William Bentley across his
doorstep at Fairview Road. It was superior class.*

Norman Parsley, the college boy.

*'Hello, Mr Bentley. I hope I'm not disturbing you. I wondered if
Derek might like to go for a walk.'*

*William Bentley hesitated. The boy in front of him was what? Seven-
teen or eighteen? Clean-cut, well-mannered. He'd never heard his
name before. He was all right, surely. Even so, the father looked up and
down the glistening wetness of Fairview Road, still anxious for the tall,
wavy-haired boy he had helped into the world nineteen summers ago.*

'It's a bit late,' he said.

*'It's only about half-past eight, Mr Bentley,' Parsley assured him.
'We won't be out long. Just a short walk.'*

Bentley looked hard at the boy. 'Wait here,' he said.

*Back in the living-room, William Bentley looked at his son. 'You can
go out with Parsley if you like,' he said, 'but promise you won't be
long.'*

*Lilian Bentley cut in, faster than she intended. 'Promise,' she said.
The urgency made Derek smile. He towered over her at six feet four
inches and put his arm round her shoulder. 'All right. Shan't be long,
Mum.' He turned to his father, still smiling. 'Thanks, Dad.'*

*He went out into the hall and collected his old brown jacket from the
stand. Norman Parsley was waiting with his foot on the doorstep.
William Bentley watched as the boys walked off together into the
night.*

*Out of sight of the Bentleys' house at No 1, around the corner in the
London Road, two other boys were waiting under the street lights:
Frank Fazey and Christopher Craig. A quicker brain than Derek*

Bentley's would have realized the ploy. Craig had sent Parsley to the Bentleys' because Parsley was a college boy. Because Craig had been turned away earlier in the day. Because Craig needed Bentley with him now. And because Norman Parsley was an armed robber who, fifteen days earlier, had burst into the house of an elderly couple and attempted to rob them at gunpoint.

It was nearly nine o'clock when the four parted company. Parsley had served his purpose. Perhaps he and Fazey had no stomach for what was to come. Craig and Bentley caught the 109 bus to Croydon. Two threepennies. It was a Sunday night. There were few people about. The church services were over and in any case the churches drew few of the faithful nowadays. The second house at the pictures was still going on. At the Streatham Astoria, where Iris Bentley worked, Betty Grable was wowing them once again in 'The Lady From The West'. At the Savoy, Croydon and the Regal, Purley, Donald Houston was shooting it out with the French police in 'My Death is a Mockery'.

They got off the bus near Tamworth Road, Craig tightening the belt of his raincoat, pulling up the collar and adjusting the brim of his trilby hat. He felt in his pocket. Metal. His fingers curled around it and in a deft movement he'd slipped the home-made knuckle-duster into Bentley's right pocket. Bentley too was armed. He had a sheath knife, slim-bladed, but without the sheath, so that the razor point tore the coat lining as he walked.

Craig pulled him back into the shadows. There it was. The butcher's shop. There was a till in there. Money. The perfect place. And Bentley had the keys. He'd lifted them the day before. Which is why Craig needed him. Which is why he had sent Norman Parsley. But wait! There was a light shining over the door. Fuckit! There was somebody there. Craig crossed the road, being as casual as he could in his Humphrey Bogart get-up. He listened at the door. Movements. Furniture being scraped. The bastard of a butcher was doing his books in readiness for Monday morning. Craig swore again and joined the taller boy. They waited. Nothing happened. No one came out. The light stayed on. What if the butcher wasn't alone? How far could Craig rely on the lad with him? Better not chance it. Try the electrical shop down the road.

Again, they stopped. Again they ducked into the shadows. All right, there were probably takings inside from the Saturday. But there was also a couple groping each other in the doorway darkness. The giggling and the rustling of clothes boded badly. They could be there for ages. And Craig and Bentley had a different kind of clandestine activity in mind.

On past the toilets they walked, up the slight gradient of Tamworth Road, past the jumble of second-hand shops at Reeves Corner. On their left, the large black outline of Barlow and Parker's confectionery warehouse held their attention. There'd be money in there, no problem. A big place like that would have lots of stuff. And lots of wages. Maybe they hadn't all been paid off on Friday. And wasn't there some rumour that the top storey was a jeweller's warehouse? Bloody marvellous. They'd have a look.

Little Pearl Ware was getting ready for bed. It was nearly quarter-past nine and there was school the next day. She pulled off her frock, looking forward to Guy Fawkes Night on Wednesday and wondering whether her dad had bought any fireworks for her.

'Mum!'

Edith Ware was putting away some clothes.

'Mum. Come and see this.'

Mrs Ware went into her daughter's bedroom. 'Time for Bedfordshire, my girl,' she said, tapping Pearl on the navy blue knickers. 'Time all little nine-year-olds were fast asleep.'

'But Mum, look at those men.'

Edith Ware shivered the nets aside. Yes, Pearl was right. There were two of them. One tall. The other shorter. She took in the familiar street furniture opposite Number 74. The street lights shone on the pavement, still glistening after the rain. Overhead a fitful moon broke now and then against the flagpole of Barlow and Parker's. The shorter man suddenly jumped up and caught the top of the expanding gate to one side of the warehouse. He hauled himself up and over and was gone. The other one hung back in the shadows of the building. He seemed to be checking the road. As a bus passed, he ducked back into the shadows again, pulling down the brim of his trilby. Then he too scrambled up and over the gate.

'John,' Mrs Ware called to her husband, 'call the police. I think there's two blokes breaking into the warehouse.'

John Ware almost nicked himself with his razor.

'Get on,' he said, but something in the urgency of his wife's words brought him up the stairs at the double.

'Look,' Edith said, 'there's one of them now. They're on the roof.'

Ware wiped the soap from his face. His wife was right.

'Stay here,' he said to his family and bolted down the stairs, grabbing his coat as he went.

Once out into the night air, he slowed up. Mustn't hurry. Don't want to alarm them and let the buggers get away. He closed the door quietly, then walked to his left out of the front, past the Eagle to where the nearest phone box stood. Once out of sight of the roof, he ran, fumbling with the heavy red door, picking up the cold bakelite.

'Emergency. Which service, caller?' the disembodied voice asked him.

'Police,' he said.

Detective Constable Frederick Fairfax sat in the less-than-comfortable CID office in the Fell Road Station. Sunday night. God! What was he doing here, typing up a report about a stolen gas meter? Maybe one day, the Commissioner of the Police of the Metropolis would get civilians to do this work. And then he could get on with being a policeman. One day. One day.

The station sergeant stuck his head round the door. It was a routine call. 'Suspects on the roof at premises in Tamworth Road,' he said, 'Barlow and Parker's warehouse.'

Fairfax got to his feet. It was a routine call. No absolute need for him to go. There'd be plenty of uniformed boys around. Maybe that was a good reason for going. Besides, it had to be better than typing up reports on stolen gas meters. He wouldn't bother with his coat. It had stopped raining now. He got to the yard at the back of the old station. An officer was manoeuvring the van. PC Harrison was crossing to the canteen. The silly bugger had come on duty without his sandwiches. Served him right. He deserved the canteen, then.

'Suspects on the roof in Tamworth Road,' Fairfax told him and they bundled into the van, Harrison's sandwiches forgotten.

It took them four minutes to reach the premises, screeching round the corners into Katharine Street, through the traffic lights into Tamworth Road. As they got there, a black wireless car pulled up behind them. At the wheel, PC Sidney Miles. Next to him, his wireless operator, James McDonald.

There were people hanging out of bedroom windows opposite shouting, 'They're up there. On the roof. On the roof.'

June Tennent had been watching television.

'Get some coal in, dear,' her mother had said.

The girl had reached the bunker by the garden wall when another police car screeched to a halt in front of her and its occupants tumbled out, scanning the skyline for any sign of the suspects.

Fairfax shinned up the expanding gate. He'd been a commando in the war, collared countless housebreakers in his day. This little one posed no problems. He found himself alone in a dark passageway. As his eyes acclimatized, he saw the brick wall of the warehouse to his right, a corrugated iron fence to his left. Ahead of him, a pair of doors that seemed to lead to stairs. He tried them. Locked. He turned back towards the gate in time to see a uniformed man heave himself up and over. It was PC James McDonald of Z Division.

McDonald couldn't see a thing at first. Then he made out the bald head and hard, square face of Fairfax. Nothing was said. McDonald watched as Fairfax began to haul himself up the nearest drain-pipe. Then he saw the footprint on the window-sill near his head. Not Fairfax's, certainly. That was how the villains had got up, too.

On the roof, Fairfax took in his surroundings. He dipped under the iron rail that ran the perimeter of the roof. To his right rose a flagpole at the front of the building. To his left as he turned towards it, a brick block, the head of the stairs whose doors had stood locked fast below him. Some feet to the right from this, four roof-lights of glass and iron, looking for all the world like miniature greenhouses. Beyond that in the almost total darkness he could make out a grey rectangular shape – the stack of a lift head. And to one side of that . . .

He walked forward between the roof-lights, aware vaguely of torch beams probing to his right and of noise growing from below, as the knot of local residents became a crowd, fascinated by the appearance of police van and patrol cars. He could see his quarry easily now. Two lads. For all one of them was a tall bastard, he wasn't very powerful-looking. They were kids.

'I am a police officer,' Fairfax shouted. 'Come out from behind that stack.'

There was a silence. To Fairfax's right and in front of him, Norman Harrison was making his way towards the roof. He'd taken his chances on another angle. He was younger than Fairfax certainly, keener perhaps. He'd run through the gardens of Nos. 25 and 26 and had dragged himself up on to the roof alongside the warehouse. It was glass and asbestos, and slippery in the wet. He'd called to Fairfax, 'Are you all right?'

The detective hadn't answered. What the bloody hell was he doing there, standing looking at a brick wall? 'Come out from behind that stack'? Harrison screwed his eyes into the darkness. Yes. Yes. There they were. Two shapes. Two men. They had their heels in the gutter that ran ahead of him and their backs to another sloping roof of glass and asbestos. He heard a young voice answer Fairfax –

'If you want us, fucking come and get us.'

Harrison braced himself. He had to get there fast. Fairfax was no slouch. He admired the bloke, knew him as a hard man. But there were two of them.

'All right,' he heard Fairfax say, 'I will.'

The detective marched forward, skirting to the right of the stack and grabbed the nearest one. It was Derek Bentley, looming over Fairfax who dragged him out into the open. He pushed him towards the staircase head. Perhaps the door there was open. He hadn't tried it. That was the best way down. The tall lad with the wavy hair wasn't putting up a fight. Fairfax wouldn't waste time. They were kids. He'd go back for the other one.

Suddenly, Bentley ripped away from him, shouting, 'Let him have it, Chris.'

Harrison was edging his way towards the stack. The roof's angle was too sharp for him to stand upright. If he ran, he'd slip sideways and probably break his neck. He probed the darkness with his torch. There was a shot, the sound reverberating around the Sunday suburbs. Harrison saw Fairfax go down, momentarily collapsing against Bentley or the roof, he couldn't tell which. He doubled his speed.

Fairfax had heard the shot, felt a searing pain in his shoulder, like a brick wall that had got up and hit him. Shocked and shaking, he instinctively caught his balance and lunged for the nearest figure as it moved away from him in the darkness. It was Bentley again and this time Fairfax hit him, smashing his head with his fist until Bentley was lying on the roof, his face pressed into the asphalt. There was another shot. The detective was in the open, bleeding, scared. He got off Bentley and dragged him to the corner of the nearest roof-light. He forced him down to a kneeling position, then frisked him, feeling metal in his pockets. First came the knuckle-duster. Craig's knuckle-duster. He pocketed it himself. Then the knife, slim-bladed like a dagger.

'That's all I've got, guv'nor,' Bentley told him, 'I haven't got a gun.'

[25]

Fairfax took stock of himself. God knew how much ammunition the bastard had behind that stack. The roof-light was only, what, four and a half feet tall at its highest point? And it was made of bloody glass. A bullet would go straight through that. He had to get off that roof.

'Look,' he hissed to Bentley, the pain beginning to get through to him, 'I'm going to work you round the roof to that escape door over there.'

He still didn't know whether that door was open or not. But it was his only chance. It meant working backwards, weaving around the other roof-light and crossing the open asphalt. Derek Bentley may have been stupid, but he wasn't that stupid –

'He'll shoot you,' he said.

But it was Harrison who was in the line of fire. Craig caught sight of the flashing torch to his left. What was that? A fireman? He had heard the fire-engine bell clanging on the ground below. They'd have ladders. They'd be able to climb up. No, it was a bloody copper. He swung to his left, holding the gun in both hands, the sawn-off Colt of which he was so proud and fired once. The bullet glanced off the asbestos to Harrison's right. The policeman froze. His heels were in the gutter. He was lying on his back, the only way he could make any progress at all. He'd seen Fairfax go down. How badly was he hurt? Surely, he couldn't cope by himself? The second bullet from Craig ricocheted off the chimney stack above Harrison's head with a whining ring that made him drop his torch. It bounced on the asbestos and slithered noisily into the gutter. Christ! That one was close. Harrison rolled back to his left. He had his truncheon in his pocket. His uniform on his back. Fourteen inches of hardwood and an eighth of an inch of serge against a bloody arsenal. He did the only thing he could do. He began the long crawl back.

June Tennent was still in the garden as the policemen brushed past her.

'Better get inside, love,' one of them grunted, 'there's a madman up there.'

They bundled her indoors and she ran up the stairs to her bedroom.

She saw Christopher Craig edging his way round the roof. He had no challenger now. Harrison was getting the fuck out of it. Good. Typical of cowardly coppers. Craig reached the corner of the roof. The crowd below was huge. There were people, pointing, gesturing. He gestured back. They remembered for years how young he looked. How his teeth gleamed in the torchlight. And they remembered the gun. He walked half-way along the roof, watching Fairfax all the time. The bald bastard wasn't giving him an inch. He was holding Bentley close to him, like a shield. If he fired now, he might hit his mate. Better leave it. He'd have another chance. He skulked back to the stack.

In the smoke and noise of the Robert Peel, the landlord, Ted Pillage, was wiping up his thousandth glass.

'There's shooting out 'ere,' a voice called round the frosted glass of the door.

'Get away,' somebody said. 'It's kids with fireworks.'

'It may be kids. But it ain't bloody fireworks. They've got guns.'

'How many of 'em?' somebody asked.

Men were on their feet, crowding towards the windows.

'Dozens of them by the sound of it.'

Ted Pillage saw the flash of a police helmet plate briefly at the doorway and heard, 'You people had better keep down . . .' before the mob surged forward, brushing the bobby aside. He'd never seen the place clear so fast. They were never that anxious to go when he called time.

It was now that Fairfax heard the scrabbling on the drainpipe. He pushed Bentley down on to the ground in the sheltering lee of the staircase head. Unless the trigger-happy bastard came back along the roof again, they'd be relatively safe here.

'Drop your gun!' he shouted.

'Come and get it!' roared Craig. This was better than a film. He'd winged one of them, driven another off. He could keep this up all night. Mechanically, he checked his pockets for ammunition.

Fairfax took a chance. There didn't seem any fight in Bentley. He'd leave him where he was and get to that pipe. He ducked behind him, peering over the rail into the total blackness of the passageway below. Grunting and sweating on the highest section of the pipe swayed McDonald, his cap askew, fighting for breath. The detective grabbed him with both hands and hauled him up over the rail. McDonald was never so glad to feel asphalt under his feet in his life.

'He got me in the shoulder,' Fairfax hissed as the three men crouched in the darkness.

'I told the silly bugger not to use it!' blurted Bentley.

The policemen ignored him. 'What sort of gun has he got, Fairy?' McDonald asked.

[27]

'It's a .45 Colt,' Bentley volunteered, 'and he's got plenty of bloody ammunition too.'

There was noise inside the staircase head. The thump of running feet. People were coming up the stairs. Reinforcements. Fairfax called out instructions. He was round to the left of those on the stairs. He heard the bar bang up. He heard the door crash open. For a brief second a uniformed figure in a peaked cap was silhouetted in the light from the stairs. There was another shot and the figure went down heavily. The hands instinctively came up to the head and he pitched forward on his face on the asphalt.

Ever known time to stand still? Ever known a second last a lifetime? For that second nothing happened. The film froze. McDonald and Fairfax looked at each other, too numbed to move. Simultaneously they shook themselves free of it, forcing the brain to jar into action, the limbs to respond. They turned the man over. It was Sidney Miles, McDonald's driver from car 7Z. His head was a mass of blood and he wasn't breathing. There was a second shot, lodging itself somewhere in the frame of the door. Fairfax and McDonald dragged the body of their comrade to the shelter of the staircase head. A dead weight. Unyielding. Unhelpful. Harrison, who had followed Miles up the stairs, leapt through the doorway. He had found Miles in the street and the driver had got the keyholder and his keys in tow. They had fumbled with the front doors, the shooting on the roof alarming them. As other officers held back the crowds, as the whole of Tamworth Road and Frith Road was lined with police cars and ambulances and fire-engines, Miles and Harrison had smashed their way into the darkened building, the keyholder darting after them, turning on lights as they went.

For a split second on the roof, Harrison looked death in the face. He had seen Miles's head explode in front of him. He had seen the body drop. Now with the truncheon in his hand he stood as though rooted to the spot, staring at the raised gun clasped in both the hands of Christopher Craig. He threw the truncheon. He saw a discarded milk bottle beside the door and he crouched and threw that. Then he saw a block of wood and he threw that too. Another bullet whipped past his ear and he flung himself around to the right, behind the staircase wall. Had he hit the bastard? With anything? He crunched down heavily against Derek Bentley who sat there shaking, staring silently at what was left of Sidney Miles.

Bob Jaggs was the last policeman from Z Division to reach the roof.

He took Fairfax's drainpipe in his stride and got to the staircase head with the others. Fairfax, McDonald, Harrison. He knew them well. But they looked strange in the half light. Wild-eyed. Afraid. Angry. And he recognized too the body of Sidney Miles. The young bastard sitting on the ground with his back to the wall he didn't know at all. All he knew was that he had helped cause this. That was all he needed to know. Who had the gun? Where was the shooting coming from? He popped his head out, like putting your toe in the water. There was a shot.

'I am Craig,' the gunman yelled at them. 'You've just given my brother twelve years. Come on you coppers. I'm only sixteen.'

Fairfax looked at the shock and bewilderment and anger on the faces of his men. They had to get Bentley out of it. There'd be dozens of coppers on the ground by now, a lot of them coming up the stairs. And there ought to be firearms. With all this shooting, somebody would have radioed for guns.

'Come on you brave coppers,' Craig taunted them. 'Think of your wives.'

Jaggs stuck his head out again and again a bullet made him tuck it in. Fairfax wanted no more nonsense like that.

'We'll get this one down the stairs,' he said, 'I'll go first. When I'm on the stairs, the rest of you follow. Put the bastard in front of you. Use him like a shield.'

In the noise and the confusion and the horror, the reality of the situation hit Derek Bentley like a sledgehammer. His fuddled brain tried to function.

'Look out, Chris,' he called, 'They're taking me down.'

Fairfax ducked into the safety of the stairs.

'Are they hurting you, Derek?' Craig called. He couldn't see in the mêlée and the dark and his gun was empty. He fumbled in his pockets, feeling the cold of the tommy gun bullets. The ones he'd filed down specially to fit. He flicked out the chamber, loading with a firm grip. Funny. He thought he'd be shaking. He wasn't.

The policemen made a rush for it, pushing Bentley into the open and then down the stairs. They stumbled over each other, hobnailed boots clattering on the concrete. At the bottom stood the square frame of Inspector Bodley, the most senior man of Z Division to have arrived by now.

'Sidney Miles, sir,' McDonald said to him.

Bodley nodded, then looked at Bentley. Funny. He didn't look like a *killer. They bundled him under the care of Sergeant Roberts into a patrol car for the four-minute ride to Croydon Police Station.*

There was a canvas bag in the office of Mr Jones, the shaken manager of Barlow and Parker who had been hastily summoned from his Sunday night fireside. Fairfax put his hand into it and pulled out a pistol. A .32 automatic. At last, an equalizer. He'd been on that roof for nearly twenty minutes. It had felt like years. He checked that it was loaded, freed the safety catch. He wasn't very good with one of these. They didn't get much practice with them, even in the Met. Maybe that would change in the future. Maybe tonight would make it change. He dashed back up the concrete steps so recently trodden by Sidney Miles whose body still lay up there under the scudding clouds and the fitful moon. Alone. Alone except for a gun crazy kid. He flashed past the anxious faces of Harrison, McDonald and Jaggs, still on the stairs, waiting for the next word. Fairfax gave no orders, no instructions. His heart was pounding in his brain, blood pumping as he ran. He'd forgotten his shoulder now. All that mattered was that he stopped that little bastard. Once and for all.

Craig was ready for him. He raised the gun. Cocked it. The door crashed back again as Fairfax reached it.

'Drop your gun!' Fairfax shouted, 'I also have a gun.'

'Come on then, copper,' snarled Craig, his blood up, 'let's have it out.'

It was still very dark. The moon had gone. What was that crash? The door? No, it sounded too metallic.

'Are you hiding behind a shield?' Craig called. 'Is it bullet proof?'

No reply. Fairfax was crouching in the doorway, choosing his moment. He didn't want to end up like Sidney Miles.

'Are we going to have a shooting match?' Craig screamed, 'It's just what I like!'

Fairfax saw his moment. He lurched forward, veering in a semicircle to avoid Craig's trajectory, firing as he went. Once. Twice. Harrison, McDonald and Jaggs were with him, scraping on the asphalt, weaving and bobbing around the roof-lights, making a bee-line for Craig who now ran to the corner of the roof.

On the ground below, two uniformed constables, Ross and Stewart, converged on that dark corner of the building where Craig swayed for a moment. They had circled the warehouse and forced their way through the tangle of scruffy gardens and sheds that led off Upper Drayton Place. Stewart saw Craig perched on the rail, his gun held out in both hands. He heard the hammer click once, then fire. Another click. And another. The damned thing had jammed. Craig rolled sideways, flinging himself over the rail. He was more than twenty feet above them. How the hell could they reach the bastard?

'Give my love to . . .' they heard him shout, but the sentence was broken by the crash of his gun through a glasshouse roof and the thud and grunt as his body bounced off the edge of a corrugated iron shed and lay in the debris of the builder's yard below.

Stewart ran for him. At him. On to him. He straddled the boy as he lay there, pinning him down in case the bastard was still armed. Still full of fight. He wasn't. He rolled over, groaning in his delirium, 'I wish I was fucking dead. I hope I've killed the fucking lot.'

Stewart looked up and saw faces peering down.

The gun battle on a Croydon roof-top was over.

It is particularly fitting that the title of this chapter is taken from the opening remarks of Mr Christmas Humphreys, the Prosecuting Counsel in the trial of Craig and Bentley, the 'trial of the century'. Like all good stories of course, it has a kernel of truth, that touch of reality which makes it feasible. It could be the plot of an episode from *The Sweeney* or *Juliet Bravo* or *The Bill.* In essence, the story you have just read, particularly the story of the roof-top events, is based on the evidence of four policemen – Frederick Fairfax, Norman Harrison, James McDonald and Robert Jaggs, the four policemen on that Croydon rooftop on the night of 2 November 1952; the four policemen who were conspicuously brave and who were decorated for their gallantry and honoured by a grateful nation.

But there was a fifth policeman on that roof. A fifth policeman whose evidence until now has not been heard. A fifth policeman whose evidence does not square with the story so far. A fifth policeman whose evidence, had it been heard, might well have saved Derek Bentley from the gallows. A doubt would not have crept into the minds of the innocent. A shadow would not have been cast over British justice. And a 'three-quarter witted boy' would be alive today.

Thirty seven years after the death of Sidney Miles; thirty six years after the execution of Derek Bentley, it is time we heard from Police Constable Claude Raymond Pain.

—— 2 ——
THE VIOLENT PLAYGROUND

Constable Claude Raymond Pain knew Derek William Bentley. Not well, it is true. But he recognized him as one of many hundreds of kids who liked to hang around on street corners. 'He was a bit dim,' Pain remembered, 'He was skylarking around near some public lavatories in Bensham Lane.' He seemed a nice boy – 'I was only having a game, guv'nor,' he had told him. He was the sort of kid whose idea of a good time was to catch a 109 bus to Croydon 'just to walk around'. Because Croydon was part of the violent playground of South London. And Derek Bentley, like Christopher Craig, was part of the delinquent sub-culture which haunted it.

A typical gazetteer of Croydon, produced in the 50's, describes it as a county borough and market town, a dormitory suburb ten miles south-east of London. East Croydon was the main line station, but there were several other stations providing arteries for the 'independent local life and industry'. The centre of the town is a long, narrow high street, a stretch of the old road from London to Brighton. Schools in the central area owed their foundation to Bishops Witgift and Tenison, the former founding in 1596 the almshouses which still stand, incongruous in this high-rise end of our own century. A Saxon settlement, Croie Dune (which means chalk hill) forged links with the archbishops of Canterbury from the time of the Norman Conquest and the old palace was used as a girls' school in the 1950's, having been vacated as an episcopal residence in 1758. Before the arrival of sea coal in London from Newcastle, Croydon supplied the capital with the bulk of its charcoal for iron-smelting. The Victorians encroached on woodland and hills and built with pride their civic monstrosities – the parish church of St John in 1867 and the Town Hall, with its imposing clock tower, some years later. Clock-making and bell founding were major industries in the earlier part of this century and there was an engineering works. Croydon airport served London as the Continental air terminus between 1920 and 1939, giving the place an air of 'glitz' and 'glamour' still present in the 50's.

The Victorians not only built and sanitized, they civilized, turning Croydon into a borough in 1888, incorporating the areas of Norbury, where Christopher Craig lived, Norwood, Addiscombe, Waddon, Selhurst, Thornton Heath, Woodside, Shirley and Addington. In the 50's, it had a mayor and corporation, and formed three borough constituencies. Its population in 1951 was 249,592 and, ironically in the case of PC Miles, had a long-standing reputation for a remarkably low death rate.

'It's all gone now. All demolished,' Claude Pain told me. Never having been to Croydon before I had a mental picture of a bleak, 1980's cityscape, a jungle of concrete and steel of the type which gives Prince Charles nightmares. When I visited the place in mid-January 1989 and emerged from the multi-storey car park at Fairfield Halls, I was struck by just that. The town centre of Croydon is at first sight a high-rise paradise. Row upon row, column upon column of 60's windows. Even the much older Technical College blends in curiously well. North End and the High Street are typical products of the last quarter of the century. Chain stores – Allders, Littlewood's, Next – have obliterated the town's identity. Christmas decorations still glinted in a tawdry, wind-damaged way in the sun of the January sales. It could have been any other town. Any other time.

Gradually, you get your eye in. The Magistrates' Court, abutting the Reference Library, is still there, a mellow brick dinosaur of Victoriana, wrapped in scaffolding and enjoying something of a facelift while I was there. Under my feet, beneath the tarmac in Fell Road, was the underground passage which linked the court to the old police station. But the police station has gone. In its place is the giant complex of Taberner House and a rather pretty park.

From Fell Road, I walked down Katharine Street and down the busy market in Surrey Street, where watered down Cockneys sell fruit and veg from disreputable stalls. Clutching my A–Z I wandered down Frith Road, noting the blend of old and new. And I was in the middle of the road when a car horn blasted me on to the pavement. It was a big, white police car from Z Division, one of several I saw during the day. Sitting next to the driver was a pretty policewoman, in the new pairings which would amaze and quite possibly appal Claude Pain. Throughout the day in Croydon, I didn't see a single policeman on foot.

Frith Road brings you out into Tamworth Road, rising in a gentle hill to your right. I should now have been standing opposite Nos. 30 and 31 and to my right should have been the premises of Barlow and Parker, but the bulldozers moved in on that in the September of 1977. What dominates now is the large Victorian John Ruskin Grammar School as was. It now appears to double as a Sports and Leisure Centre and offices for a number of large and anonymous international companies. The Tamworth Arms pub is still there, full to the gunwales with old men watching Saturday afternoon sport on the telly. Further down to my left, the Eagle still stands and the extraordinary monopoly of Reeves Corner, where the upholstery store first opened in 1867 and seems to have bought up all the property in sight. It was here that Derek Bentley worked happily for Mr Hutchins before his back trouble lost him his job. From here, and from the roof of Barlow and Parker, the parish church of St John is clearly visible.

I walked back past the school and caught my breath for a moment. Above the high wall, on the roof of outbuildings, stand four roof-lights, identical with the ones on *the* roof-top thirty-seven years ago. But they are on the wrong roof, ten feet too low and a hundred yards to the left. I walked down Drayton Road and turned left into Lower Drayton Place. Here I stood rooted to the spot. The houses are still there, tiny terraces of a century ago, with small, decrepit back gardens, utterly unchanged since 1952. Only, once again, these are the wrong gardens, the wrong houses and the brick wall and sloping roof rising ahead belong to the New Life Christian Centre, which, a workman told me, is no more than ten years old.

The perimeter of the area is still marked – by the houses in Drayton Road, the Tamworth Arms and the school and No. 83, decaying like an old, bad tooth in a row of gleaming enamel dentures. The 'dentures' are now a garage and multi-storey car park, where once stood the Sir Robert Peel pub, whose landlord had witnessed the roof-top incident and where once stood the home of John and Edith Ware, whose little girl had seen two young men acting suspiciously.

On the site of the warehouse itself, a 70's creation now stands. A tight little formation of modern houses, attractive in their mellow red-brick. They stretch to the Waddon New Road and the railway line beyond, swallowing up entirely what was Upper Drayton Place, where PCs Stewart and Ross had raced towards the end of the gun battle.

'Nothing beside remains.'

What the typical gazetteer of Croydon does not mention is the existence of a substratum of society, almost an anti-society, composed largely of young people and dominated in the still-sexist 1950's by young males.

A great deal of psychological and sociological research has been carried out into crime over the last forty years, particularly into the phenomenon associated with the 50's, that of juvenile delinquency. Most of this research has centred on American juveniles and American crime, and, in the 50's at any rate, the parallels were slim. In 1963, a *daily* crime toll in New York City was something like this – one murder, twenty-seven felonious assaults, three rapes, one hundred and forty burglaries, sixty-nine grand larcenies and more. John Barron Mays, Professor of Social Science at Liverpool University in the early 60's, quite rightly says 'even London seems like a kindergarten by comparison'.

It is this kindergarten, this adventure playground strewn with violence and the opportunities for violence, which may provide the clues to what *really* happened on that Croydon roof-top thirty-seven years ago. And we have to see it all in context.

In terms of society, though not in law, both Christopher Craig and Derek Bentley were children in November 1952. How much *emotionally* Bentley had aged by 28 January 1953 we shall never know. The way we treat children has changed. The society created by adults creates conflicting and confusing values and ideals for them. On the one hand, Christopher Craig could not vote in 1952; neither could Derek Bentley – the age of majority was twenty-one. Yet, they had been at work (or in Bentley's case, out of it) since they were fifteen. And the law presumed they were old enough to stand trial and to be responsible for their actions because they were over fourteen. Psychologists might well argue that the age of rationalism – of knowing right from wrong, for example – hits most people at the age of seven. And what, I wonder, was the mental and moral age of Derek Bentley, with his IQ hovering somewhere around 66 and his reading age of 4½?

Two things need to be accepted if we are to understand the Craigs and Bentleys of this world and the society which bred them. First, crime is normal. Whether you accept a literal interpretation of the Bible, with its original sin concept (and the first murder, that of Abel by Cain, followed soon after) or whether you take a more humanist, evolutionary stance, a glance at the history of mankind shows that crime is as old as society itself. The fact that we do not all engage in it does not make it abnormal. But *is* it a fact that we do not all engage in it? The unpaid television licence, the library book you forgot to return, the double yellow lines you parked on this morning – these are all examples of 'crimes'. They are not indictable crimes or serious offences and very few people would throw up their hands in horror and say that the country was going to the dogs as a result of them. But, technically, they are examples of law-breaking. *And we are all guilty of them.*

The second thing to grasp is that there are strong tendencies in children, which, if not controlled and channelled, will lead to a lawless and vicious collapse of society. As I am writing this, a thirteen-year-old has been found guilty of the murder of a two-year-old girl. He is the youngest boy (twelve at the time of the incident) to be convicted of murder in modern times. A recent editorial in the *Daily Mail* made comment on this. In words reminiscent of John Parris's attempt to 'sweeten' the character of Christopher Craig, Mary Kenny of the *Mail* invited us to look at the innocent face, the freckles, the engaging smile. How could anyone believe a little boy – 'he might be yours or mine', writes Mrs Kenny – capable of such monstrosity, suffocating a toddler in the mud prior to sexually assaulting her? Again, the unpalatable fact is that most of us, as children, *are* capable of it. It is only the 'civilizing' agencies of adulthood that make it less likely.

John Mays remembers his own schooldays. John Parris, defending Craig at the Old Bailey, urged the jury to do the same thing. Mays remembers deliberately scaling dangerous heights overhanging the sea, even though he could not swim and, even if he had been able to, would have been smashed to lifelessness by the power of the surge hitting the rocks. As a child I did exactly the same thing myself. Other children do it by playing 'chicken' – darting in front of oncoming cars or playing on railway lines. This is not a death wish, but it is certainly not the act of a rational, thinking human being. It is merely the manifestation of youth without experience.

'Any boy,' wrote Mays, 'must know at first hand the dread of destruction. He must hang over his own precipice alone and feel his blood race . . .'

And he goes on to make the point that the underprivileged boy, especially from an urban area, as it might be Croydon, must find outlets for this psychological craving within his own environment: 'For the slum boy who has what the Services call "guts", the side of the warehouse is his mountain chasm . . . Nightwatchmen, patrolling

police and shopkeepers are worthy antagonists to test his steel against
. . .' For the wealthy and the privileged, the opportunity is golden and
boyhood lasts for ever. So Francis Chichester, Chris Bonnington and
Ranulph Fiennes are just so many latter-day Peter Pans. They climb
mountains and face ice, snow and sea 'because they are there'. For
boys like Christopher Craig and Derek Bentley – and he most certainly
was a boy who never grew up – there was an element of something else.

John Mays admits to being horrified that most of his youth club lads
in Liverpool in the early 60's had been involved in crime of one sort
or another – shoplifting, stealing from lorries, breaking and entering.
These were lads Mays considered 'good': that is, morally aware and
responsible teenaged citizens. That they had never been caught did not
alter the fact that they were anything but moral. When he questioned
them, it became apparent that the motive usually present in adult
crimes of theft – gain – was almost wholly lacking. The boys did it for
fun, for the electric thrill of entering a sealed building in the dark, of
lying motionless under a window as a nightwatchman passed, of
running down the road delirious with happiness *just because you've
done it*. It was these confessions that made Mays think back to his own
childhood.

So we are all capable of crime, some of it serious and we are doubly
capable of it as children. But very few of us end our childhood by
shooting at policemen on a warehouse roof. What else was it about
Craig and Bentley?

The first bomb fell on Croydon airport on 15 August 1940. As
London's leading airport at that time, it came in for a great deal of
attention from the Luftwaffe and suffered doubly in the sense that it
was a target in the early phase of the Battle of Britain, when airfields
were hit, and also in the later phases when London in general was the
focus of the 'blitz' in order to sap civilian morale. Nor was the
bombing confined to 1940. Croydon was the worst hit of all London
boroughs by the 'doodlebugs', V1 and V2 rockets, 142 falling in the
area by the summer of 1945.

Christopher Craig and Derek Bentley were nine and twelve respect-
ively when the war ended. All too little research has been done into the
problem of children whose lives have been dislocated by war, indeed
on the effects on society generally. But it is generally accepted that
because of the circumstances of war, society came to tolerate a new

norm of violence. It was in 1945, as the Allied armies liberated Europe, that the full horror of the concentration camps like Dachau, Auschwitz and Buchenwald came to light. It was in 1945 that the world began to count the cost, in terms of human life and misery, of allowing fanaticism to grow unchecked in politics.

There is particular evidence that small children who have endured bombing raids (Bentley was twice dug out from the shattered debris of his home), evacuation, blackout, rationing and the daily threat of death, emerged disturbed and disturbing. A Government paper produced by Leslie Wilkins in 1961 called *Delinquent Generations* proved that boys born between 1935 and 1942 (in other words, Christopher Craig) 'have been exceptionally criminal'. Those who were four or five during bombing raids (in other words, Christopher Craig) were the most delinquent of all.

'There is a strong prima facie case' wrote Mays, 'for connecting the general upset in family and social life during the war years with the antisocial behaviour of young people who, at a particularly susceptible and sensitive stage of their psychological development, had to endure exceptionally adverse conditions.'

Interestingly, nothing was made of this fact in the trial of Craig and Bentley. Perhaps because the adults in the case were themselves too close to the age of violence. Perhaps this kind of psychological research was deemed irrelevant to the roof-top issues. Certainly Lord Goddard, who tried the case, would have no truck, for example, with the pernicious effects of cinema and juvenile literature: 'Now let us put out of our minds in this case any question of films or comics or literature of that sort.'

It is difficult to see why Parris and Cassels, defending Bentley, didn't make more of the shattered youth of their defendants. Such arguments would certainly have been new and were not then fashionable, but they were at least as pertinent as the respective defences that were put forward.

What kind of society existed for the Craig and Bentley boys in the aftermath of war? Physically, the area was scarred by debris. There were holes in the ground and wildernesses of weedy rubble where once had been homes and gardens. The cosy little world of the Croydon gazetteer ignores this entirely. It was a temporary aberration that would go. And anyway, the town planners of the 60's and 70's and 80's have done a far more convincing job in terms of wholesale destruction than anything achieved by Hitler's Luftwaffe.

It was the age of austerity. The sense of achievement and euphoria in defeating Germany and Japan left a bitter taste, made more bitter by the fact that nearly everything was still rationed and some of it still would be at the time of the Craig and Bentley case. Petrol, clothes and most foodstuffs sold at two or three times the usual price, but people survived. And they survived because of the existence of the Black Market, of people who knew people who knew people, and were able to 'fiddle' as the jargon went, with the help of an army of 'spivs' who had all the angles. Among the specifics of crime, Post Office frauds, lead-stealing from church roofs and smash and grab raids increased enormously. Even the Victoria and Albert Museum was burgled in 1948 and two swords worth the then astronomical sum of £15,000 were stolen.

But was the post-war society any worse than pre-war? In terms of crime figures, yes, it was, and we see a convincing rise here which is usually called a crime wave. It did not help that the Metropolitan Police Force, whose relatively new Z Division did their best to cope with Croydon, was drastically under strength. So in the period 1938–59 the amount of reported crime had more than doubled, although the population increase was only 10%. Crimes of violence against the person had increased fivefold; crimes like breaking and entering two and a half times. What these figures do not tell us is whether the number of crimes had increased or the number of criminals. In other words, were a relatively fixed number of criminals carrying out, and presumably getting away with, more crimes per head? Some commentators on the period are of the opinion that it was the criminals who were increasing, lured into casual and perhaps habitual crime by the temptations and privations of the time. Certainly, the figures suggest that 'the older teenagers are unusually delinquent and that their offences are more aggressive in nature than they used to be' (Mays). For instance, crimes of breaking and entering in the period committed by males in the 17–21 age group increased fourfold; crimes of violence against the person by the same age group, tenfold.

It is true, of course, that there are 'lies, damned lies and statistics' and crime figures can be all things to all men. For example, they can change dramatically if there are sudden changes in the law – as there were in the emergency situation of wartime. So, black market operations, refusal to obey blackout regulations and conscientious objection, for instance, became offences against the state and pushed crime figures up. Similarly, changes in the attitude of the public will alter the figures. Although evidence is as yet unclear, it seems likely that the huge increase in alleged child abuse cases in the 80's has more to do with the publicity given to the problem by Esther Rantzen on prime-time television than to a genuine increase in molestation. Finally, alterations in the pattern of police procedures will also alter figures. The classic example of this belongs to the 30's when Lord Trenchard took over as Commissioner of the Metropolitan Police. To increase efficiency, he ordered a new means of recording crime – the 'crimes reported' and 'suspected stolen' figures to be kept in one book. Consequently the larceny figures for 1931 in the Metropolitan area stand at 9,534 and for 1932 at an astonishing 34,783! There had been no crime wave, no sudden upsurge in immorality, merely a different type of bookkeeping.

Nevertheless, even taking into account the dubious nature of crime statistics, most authorities accept that they are only the 'tip of the iceberg' and that far more crime occurs than is actually reported; and that society post-war was more criminal, certainly more immoral, than pre-war. But the very fact that the Craig and Bentley case caused the sensation it did is proof that the violence associated with the killing of a policeman could still rock a nation, even a nation that had so recently endured six years of war. The figures indisputably show in fact that the 'crime wave' was declining by the end of 1952.

A view of the Croydon of Craig and Bentley was given to me by Raymond Pain, son of the police constable whose evidence forms the basis of this book. Young Pain was a police cadet at the time, one of that short-lived group formed by Sir Harold Scott, the then Commissioner of the Metropolitan Police. Ray Pain is the same age as Christopher Craig. They walked the same streets. How far they grew up in the same shadows is difficult to say. Pain remembers gangs without violence. They collected on street corners, eyeing the girls, trying to outdo each other in the luridness of their 'kipper' ties. Occasionally, the police would raid the cinemas (Croydon was awash with cinemas) and kick out the under-age courting couples from the back rows. Croydon was a great place to be. You felt safe. Iris Bentley remembers it like that too.

A little later a slightly different picture emerges from a friend called Terry, who was born in the same Mayday hospital as the body of Sidney Miles was taken to after the shooting. He attended Tavistock School, notorious in the area for being a rough establishment. It was renowned for its skill at boxing and Terry suggested to me that this was because of constant fisticuffs between pupils and teachers! The police were there most weeks. He lived in a prefab, the Government's answer to the bomb damage in the area, in Castle Hill Crescent. He remembers the house gleaming with brassware. The family moved away but were back in Croydon by the time Terry was five (the year before the Craig and Bentley case). As he grew up he became part of that world of danger to which John Mays refers: the danger phase, when criminal activity is likely to happen, between eight and fifteen. For Terry, a typical thirteen-year-old of his times, it was 'a great place to live'. Children of his age frequently went to school drunk, break-ins were common, fights between gangs a daily – and nightly – event.

The magic of the area ran all through Terry's conversation. Croydon was the site of the last public gallows in England. And the last tram ran past the Davis theatre from South Croydon to Thornton Heath Pond. In the mid-50's there were still huge, derelict tenements, ideal for kids intent on smashing windows. Behind Allders' store in Kennard's Arcade off George Street was the fast vanishing world of Edwardiana, elegant shopfronts and wall paintings, a circular riding-school in the basement and a private zoo with monkeys and parakeets. The Classic Cinema in the streets above had a tea trolley and biscuits brought round by the usherette in the interval.

It was interesting, listening to Terry, to hear how frequently Tamworth Road arose. One of his earliest memories is of a bad car crash at Reeves Corner, down the road from the Barlow and Parker warehouse, when his dad hauled a man from a vehicle mangled by a trolleybus. As a fourteen-year-old apprentice he worked around the corner from the warehouse.

Terence Morris uses Croydon for a sociological study in his *The Criminal Area*, written in 1957. In it he poses the interesting idea of criminal patterns of behaviour passed on from one generation to the next within a certain area, just as other forms of culture are passed on. Terry admitted to me that he was often on the fringes of trouble – nothing serious, but an uncle of his was in and out of prison all the time. The fringe criminal activity that exercised the uncle was one which was only developing at the end of the 50's and so its relevance to Craig and Bentley may seem slight. It is, however, part of the development of the violent playground and needs, I feel, to be discussed. David Yallop, another contemporary of Craig, spent his youth only a bus ride away in South London, and describes the stabbing to death of John Beckley on Clapham Common in July

1953. Yallop saw the seventeen-year-old boy lying on the pavement, his white shirt stained red. He had been slashed and stabbed nine times. This was perhaps the first of the 'Teddy Boy' killings but it was by no means the last.

The 'peer group culture' of the gangs has been studied more closely in America than in Britain. Frederic Trasher, writing in the 30's, paints the scene:

> [The gang] is characterised by the following types of behaviour: meeting face to face, milling, movement through space as a unit, conflict and planning. The result of this collective behaviour is the development of tradition, unreflective internal structure, *esprit de corps*, solidarity, morale, group awareness and attachment to a local territory.

Terry remembers that the violence of the gangs flared and died away in the areas of West Croydon, Reeves Corner and Thornton Heath. The flick-knives and the chains, infinitely more sinister and more deadly than the weapons cradled with fascination by Lord Goddard in his summing up at the trial, were the everyday armaments of these groups. They wore thick suede Brothel Creepers or cramping winklepickers on their feet; long, velvet-collared jackets and shoestring ties, and they combed their hair backwards in an attempt to emulate Tony Curtis or Elvis Presley. Most of Terry's contemporaries spent their evenings hanging around the toilets, like those in the Tamworth Road, waiting to harass and menace 'queers' who might also go there in search of 'rough trade'. Or they picked on the then small and beleaguered immigrant community for a spot of 'Paki bashing'. Interestingly, both Ray Pain and Terry summed up the Croydon of their adolescence in the same way – 'You were safe'. Unless, that is, you were black or homosexual.

Issues of gang warfare – the cult of Rock 'n' Roll, the fear of racial and sexual aberration – do not at first seem to fit Craig and Bentley, although Bentley claimed that Craig had a gang of at least five or six. It is this image that Francis Selwyn has misread in *Gangland*. His description of the boys' clothes is straight out of the Teddy Boy era of five or six years later. Craig in his 'smart' outfit looks ludicrous today – the outsize dark trenchcoat, the wide trousers with turn-ups, the trilby. Bentley looks more dapper in pinstriped suit and 'kipper' tie. The press at the time made something of Craig's 'gang', but if it existed beyond the bravado of his swaggering persona, it was composed of college boys like Norman Parsley, nonentities like Frank Fazey and two or three thirteen-year-old girls. Craig and Bentley lived in a peculiar twilight world rather akin to prehistory. Derek Bentley died eighteen months or so before the film *Blackboard Jungle* was shown in British cinemas. And that film, dismissed by a number of film critics then and since, has become seminal, because it linked for ever the haunting 'Rock Around the Clock' which was its theme tune and the violence of anti-establishment, symbolized by the flick-knife.

Even in the musical sense, Craig and Bentley were in a twilight world. The 'official' music, courtesy of the Light Programme on the radio, was still essentially big band, although the era of the ballad had dawned. Names like Perry Como, Vic Damone and Dean Martin emerged, but as Tony Palmer points out in *All You Need Is Love*, they were very similar to the pre-war crooners like Bing Crosby: 'Only one gave a hint of the pandemonium just around the corner: the Million Dollar Teardrop, the self-styled Nabob of Sob, Johnnie Ray.' Like Derek Bentley, Ray fell on his head as a child. The accident left Bentley an epileptic – it helped make Ray a millionaire. Even so, Ray was an American and his records took time to reach the British markets and still longer to reach the ultra-conservative British radio.

The delinquents who formed the Teddy Boy gangs of the mid and late 50's were anti-society for the hell of it. They saw themselves at war with the law-abiding majority in society because, as Albert K. Cohen noted in *Delinquent Boys* (1956), they *knew* they were socially disadvantaged, that they lacked good schools, good homes, and so created a substitute society instead. Terence Morris in his study of Croydon argues that this subculture, this substitute society, is basically proletarian and lower income. A boy from this background is likely to be 'less inhibited and more spontaneous than his middle-class counterpart . . . easily irritated and erupts more readily into delinquency.'

Even so, richer boys from 'better' homes – boys like Christopher Craig himself, perhaps, or Norman Parsley – often find themselves dragged into this substitute society, which is anti-law and anti-police. The *Lancet* of 4 June 1960 made this interesting observation on class and violence. What was the difference, it asked, between a 'Teds' carve up' and the weekend activities of the average middle-class rugger team, with the assault and grievous bodily harm of the scrum, the indecent exposure of the communal bath, the drunken and disorderly behaviour of the visit to the pub, the singing of obscene songs and the blatant larceny of 'collecting' inn signs and road names on the way home? What indeed? Yet the snobbery of the thing remains. Christopher Craig's father was an ex-officer, a chief cashier at a bank, and Lord Goddard had no doubt that Craig Junior came from a good home. Derek Bentley's father worked for the electricity board, altogether from a humbler walk of life – 'It is dreadful to think that two lads, one [Craig] at any rate, coming, and I dare say the other, from decent homes, should with arms of this sort go out in these days to carry out unlawful enterprises . . .'* What contempt is concealed, I wonder, in that afterthought, 'and I dare say the other'?

Fenton Bresler, in his biography of Lord Goddard, lifts snobbery to loftier levels altogether: '. . . On the 1st November 1952 Craig committed . . . his first armed robbery . . . his sixteen-year-old accomplice was not Derek Bentley, but a much brighter, local grammar school boy whom it is not now necessary to name.' For the record, his name was Norman Parsley, one of those richer, more privileged kids drawn by whatever magnetism into the delinquent subculture. Throughout the case, the sense of 'snobbery with violence' never quite goes away. The slur on Bentley's working-class origins is evident from Goddard, as we have seen; from Cassels, who calls him 'Bentley' rather than 'Derek'; and from Matheson, the medical officer who examined him in Brixton prison before the trial.

On Sunday, 2 November 1952, Christopher Craig went to see *My Death is a Mockery*, with its shoot-out sequence between the hero and the police. Dismiss it though he did at the trial, there can be no doubt that the Lord Chief Justice of England was out of joint with the times when he failed to recognize the impact of the cinema on the lives of the Craig/Bentley generation.

Christopher Craig was able to indulge himself in this fantasy world because he went to the pictures alone or with friends of his own age. There was no parental guidance; no one to point out the make-believe of the genre. And his favourite genre was the gangster film. Here the lines of morality were not clear-cut. Often, the hero was himself a criminal and the audience was faced with a choice of men – perhaps Bogart, Cagney or Raft – who all came from the wrong side of the tracks and to whom lawlessness was a way of life. It is not the reformed

* *Notable British Trials: the Trial of Craig and Bentley* London 1954

do-gooder priest, Pat O'Brien, one remembers from Warner Brothers' *Angels With Dirty Faces* but the magnetic personality of small-time crook Jimmy Cagney. Yes, he plays the coward on his way to the electric chair (where death usually takes at least four minutes) because O'Brien has asked him to, so that he will not appear a hero to the Dead End Kids of O'Brien's boys' club. But we, the cinema audience, know it is a sham, that Cagney is really totally fearless. And the last screaming seconds of Cagney's shadow struggling and kicking in terror are made more horrific because we sense that society is to blame, that the forces of the establishment have conspired to murder a man who is a 'nice guy' with whom we can all identify. Similarly, the mother-fixated Cagney, spraying the police with machine-gun bullets on the *top of a roof* in 'White Heat', brings out, if not our admiration, at least our sympathy. We can even feel a little for Edward G. Robinson, dying in a hail of bullets in *Little Caesar* – 'Mother of God, is this the end of Ricco?'

It was this confused tradition of morality, against a background of violence in which the police and the forces of authority are seen as the villains and the enemy, which underscored the outlook of dislocated youths like Craig. Let Lord Goddard dismiss it as much as he liked, research undertaken over the last twenty years – on films far more violent than anything Craig watched – has proved how all-pervading and pernicious they are. Studies by criminologists like Cressey and Thresher had shown as early as 1933 that delinquents attended the cinema more frequently than other children; as Craig said at his trial, 'A lot of times; three or four times a week.'

It is pointless more recent writers like Francis Selwyn reminding us that *My Death is a Mockery* starred Donald Houston and Bill Kerr, the one a handsome, lightweight leading man and the other a comedian. Such comments are made with the hindsight of the 'video nasty' generation. The point is that films like that *did* have a pernicious effect on their young, impressionable audiences. There was a whole series of trashy American and pseudo-American films which they went to see. And it is salutary to remember that the average cinema-goer, like the average jury member, has a surprisingly limited intellect, roughly equivalent, in now-outdated educational terms, with CSE Grade 4. Such cinema-goers do not marvel at the film's techniques, the acting ability of the cast, the purity of adaptation from book to screen. They *do*, however, get a message – and it's often the wrong one. For gullible people, for naïve people, for young people, what appears on the screen

[45]

is not entertainment: it is an extension of reality. Life – and death – are really like that. So Craig swaggered around the streets. He wore trenchcoat and trilby, like Cagney and Bogart. He drawled in pseudo-American accents. And he carried weapons. *Time Magazine* said of *White Heat*, released in 1949: 'In the hurtling tabloid traditions of the gangster movies of the 30's, but its matter-of-fact violence is a new post-war style.'

To *Time Magazine* at least, violence post-war had become matter-of-fact. It was, by many people, taken for granted. And the antagonism between good and evil, between society and the alternative society of the violent playground, was shown nowhere better than in Michael Relph's *The Blue Lamp*, also in 1949. The hysterical, quaking yet macho Dirk Bogarde, smoking frenetically and desperately trying to keep up his bravado, confronts quiet, sensible, pleasant police constable Jack Warner in the course of an armed robbery (of a cinema, ironically) and shoots him dead. It could almost have been a blueprint for Craig and Miles. The film was used as a training vehicle for police cadets, spawned a television series that ran intermittently for twenty-one years, and reached a new point in realism for the British cinema, essentially stuck in the quaint, nostalgic Ealing mould, with the single line: 'We're on to the bastard who shot George Dixon.'

When Constable Claude Pain talked to me about his experience on the Croydon roof-top, he admitted to being shocked by Craig's language. When he quoted him saying 'Come on, you bastards,' he did so in hushed tones. It was a Sunday when he spoke to me, as it had been a Sunday when Craig spoke to him. He was a guest in my house. He didn't want his wife or mine to hear it, I suspect. Claude Pain, like George Dixon, was a copper of the old school. It was this element of the alternative society that shocked him perhaps more than anything else.

It was not only the cinema that had an effect on Craig and Bentley. Because they were both unable to read fluently, they both 'read' comics. Research by the criminologist Hoult in 1949 proved that juvenile delinquents had a higher exposure to this sort of literature than other children. Niven Craig senior said in court of his son's reading habits: 'I think the only books he knows anything about are the books of Enid Blyton that he gets other people to read to him.'

One wonders how much mileage young Craig got out of the

parochial, dim-witted PC Plod! Comics in particular appealed to children of limited reading ability because they relied – and rely – on the visual impact, punctuated occasionally by the simple word. Some of these comics, mostly imported from America and dominated by gangsterdom, were so pernicious that they had been banned from Britain by 1955. In *The Seduction of the Innocent*, the author, Dr Frederic Wertham, writes: 'The world of the comic books is the world of the strong, the ruthless, the bluffer, the shrewd deceiver, the torturer and the thief . . . hostility and hate set the pace of almost every story.'

Wertham is the only American to comment on the Craig and Bentley case. He does not in fact mention either by name, but quotes Niven Craig on his son's reading habits and his 'word blindness' (dyslexia). Wertham carries several pages relating IQ to reading matter and makes his point cogently enough. Francis Selwyn says that Wertham's researches were made obsolete by the end of the 50's, when later psychologists reported that violence of the sado-sexual-masochistic type did not have an effect on children. He also reminds us that Craig's reading matter was the bland Enid Blyton, which could not have corrupted anybody. Again, this depends on the evidence you choose to accept. Wertham cites dozens of cases far more horrific than that of Christopher Craig, of American children committing suicide and murder because of the undesirable influence of violent comics. People like Selwyn – and people like Goddard – will always choose to ignore such influences, whatever the evidence. And Niven Craig was only aware of his son's reading habits when under the eye of his family. The same father found his murderous son 'very gentle'.

Derek Bentley's persona is so different from that of Craig that I accept fully that the only comics which he enjoyed were the *Beano* and the *Dandy*. He was also addicted to Rupert Bear.

The final influence on the young, impressionable Craig was that of the availability of weapons. Before I came to write this book, my only tangible connection with the case was slight but telling. I had just celebrated my third birthday when the roof-top shooting took place and because of it, my parents vowed that I would never own a gun, even a toy one. They were thwarted in this by a family friend who bought me a revolver. I can remember that gun very vividly. It didn't actually revolve at all, but its yellow trigger and hammer were separate from its red body, so it must, I suppose, have clicked. I loved that gun.

It was plastic and even when it was chewed and broken and had fallen apart, the two halves became two guns.

Our attitude to weapons has changed. All that precluded me from obtaining a real gun in my teens was the cost, although I am sure my parents would have had something to say on the matter. As I write this, my eight-year-old son is rushing around the garden, firing his caps off from his toy Remington .44. I wonder how far he is removed from Christopher Craig? There is no doubt that the 'gun culture' phenomenon reached crisis point in 1987 when Michael Ryan, for no apparent reason, blasted sixteen people to death in the peaceful provincial town of Hungerford. Questions were asked; rifle clubs suspected; video nasties deplored. Fittingly, on Armistice Day 1988, the *Daily Mail* carried the news that toy gun sales had slumped in the shops, to the extent that manufacturers reckoned to have lost £10 million. Hamley's, the country's leading toy shop, has a policy of hiding the guns away as discreetly as possible. Yet in many ways, Ryan's escapade was only an extension of Craig's shoot-out. In many ways, only the reality of which my son's activity today is the make-believe. Yet to Craig certainly and to Bentley possibly, what was the reality and what was the make-believe? How could they differentiate? The law in 1952 decided they could. Perhaps nowdays we would not be too sure.

And when John Parris reminded the jury of their boyhoods – 'Would not you have been delighted to get your hands on a revolver that really worked? And even if you could not, do you not remember the sort of pistols that had blanks in them and made a great deal of noise?' – he was simply summing up generations of stereotypical sexism. 'Thus little boys' writes Mays, 'are encouraged to be rough, to play with guns and to stage mock battles.'

The difference, of course – and it is a crucial difference – is that Christopher Craig and Michael Ryan had access to the real thing, which, for reasons of expense or legality, most of us do not. No doubt the trophies which came home in the bottom of returning soldiers' kitbags in 1945 included quite a vast number of firearms. Niven Craig senior was ex-army. He was a hero of the First World War and owned many guns himself. His son inherited what amounted to an obsession with firearms, first firing an antique weapon, owning between forty and fifty and taking them to school and to work, to impress his friends. No doubt they were impressed. And no doubt Derek Bentley and others became used to this situation, so that for Craig to carry a gun, though perhaps bizarre to outsiders, became regarded as the norm. In my own schooldays, a friend of mine brought guns to school, not often, but occasionally, and no one recoiled in horror or amazement.

As for Craig's knuckleduster and his and Bentley's knives, again these must be seen in context. 'Did you not, on occasions,' Parris asked the jury, 'carry most sinister-looking knives?' One of the favourite games of my childhood was one called 'the splits' in which two people faced each other and one threw a knife into the ground to the right or left of the other. The second person would then have to spread his feet until his foot covered the spot where the blade had embedded itself. If you hit the ground dead centre between your opponent's feet you were allowed to stand upright again. I shudder now at the prospect of what could have happened if a careless or malicious throw had driven the blade through a foot, but as a careless, irresponsible child, I didn't think of that. No child did. Would Lord Goddard, I wonder, have been so outraged by the large sheath knife Craig carried if Craig had been a Boy Scout? And the comment of the Lord Chief Justice on the knuckleduster is interesting: 'You have got a spike with which you can jab anybody who comes at you; if the blow with the steel is not enough, you have got this spike at the side to jab . . . it is a shocking weapon.'* Exactly the kind of weapon that Dr Wertham says American kids made – and used – in their hundreds.

Derek William Bentley was born at 11.30 p.m. on 30 June 1933, at home, as was still the custom then. Home was a squalid two-roomed flat at 13, Surrey Row, Blackfriars, south of the river, and conditions were so cramped that his elder sister Joan was farmed out to a grandmother. The house was due for demolition, so damp that the plaster and brickwork were crumbling and the whole edifice seemed held together with tarpaulin and sheets of corrugated iron. A second sister, Iris, was two at the time of Derek's birth. A completely unexpected twin brother, born several hours after Derek, died two hours later.

If you believe in the Fates, then they certainly had it in for Derek Bentley. The baby had to be rushed to Guy's Hospital within hours of birth. Bronchial pneumonia was diagnosed, perhaps because he had been left unattended in the panic over the second birth. His father William had some first aid skill and a midwifery diploma from the St John Ambulance Association. He helped deliver both babies. Only

---

* *Notable British Trials* op. cit.

constant care and a series of blood transfusions saved Derek's life. When he was four and playing with older children on a lorry of pulp rolls destined for the Fleet Street presses, he fell fifteen feet and landed on his head. Iris, who was playing with him, has carried the guilt of this all her life. He was once again rushed to Guy's and his parents were told that the blow had caused an epileptic fit and that it was unlikely he would ever recover entirely. When he was seven, a German bomb demolished the air raid shelter where the family was hiding. Soon after, Derek's sister Joan, his grandmother and aunt were all killed in the same way. William Bentley was senior Air Raid Warden for the street.

'I did not know it at the time,' he wrote years later, 'but I actually brought out the dead body of my own daughter. She was unrecognizable. At the identification later, I remember the clothes.'

The little boy became withdrawn, both because of the fits and the loss of his sister, to whom he had been very close. When he was eleven in September 1944 a 'doodle-bug' hit the Bentleys' flat and concrete and tiles rained in on the boy as he lay asleep. After this, the headaches increased in number and severity.

Bentley's education was typical of a child of his working-class background who had the misfortune to be born when he did. In keeping with the more progressive London boroughs, he began nursery school at the age of three in the Friar Street Elementary School, virtually next door to the family home, by this time in Webber Street. His first day at school, like that of many other kids, was a disaster, but he would not settle down. The screaming continued. Only when Iris was allowed to sit with him was he content. He began well, but the lorry accident made him a changed lad. Even so, his teachers were pleased with his progress and he took part in a Nativity play.

By 1940 the school was closed because of bomb damage and the Bentley family, distraught over the loss of its women, moved to the rather less targeted area of Edgware. From August 1941 to December 1943 Bentley attended Camrose Avenue School and the family moved back in the spring of '44 to the Blackfriars area, ironically because the house in Edgware had been destroyed by a 'doodle-bug'. At the age of eleven, Bentley went to the John Ruskin School in Walworth where his illiteracy soon became obvious. Further visits to the family doctor proved as pointless as earlier ones had been. 'Wartime conditions' was the doctor's shrugged diagnosis. In the last year of the war, the Bentleys moved again, this time to Norbury.

It didn't help that William Bentley was called up to join the Catering Corps. It wasn't front-line fighting, but it took Derek's dad away from him and in a letter William was to remember that dark January nine years later, his wife Lilian wrote to say 'Poor little Derek is a lost soul'. The family were almost destitute until William obtained compassionate leave, £10 from a kind Commanding Officer and £25 from the Corps Welfare Fund. He went home to them and noticed that little Derek's skin was a bluish colour, as it had been after his birth; and the headaches had worsened again.

They had had four homes in twelve years. The headmaster of Norbury Manor School, which Bentley now attended, gave an interview in a local newspaper article which is of particular interest in view of the violent playground and the attitude of the authorities towards the rising crime rate:

> 'We use the cane . . . we are still old-fashioned enough to believe that if a boy kicks over the traces then he should be made to realize that punishment is going to be swift and automatic. I don't think I can recall one boy who has resented corporal punishment . . . a couple of good handers and it is all over . . .*

As an alien from a different part of London, as a lad with an obvious disability, he became the butt of cruel jokes and jibes. In this school he was without Iris, for the first time. She was now at work. And he was not physically tough enough to stop the cruelty with his fists. He did what most children do who, for whatever reason, find school impossible. He simply didn't go. In an unusual burst of anger and desperation, he said to his father one day: 'Why do they hate me? I want to be like all the others. I want to read the history books and write essays, but I can't! I can't!'

The modern education system with its long back-up of pastoral care didn't exist in 1946, ironically only two years after the most important education act of the century. The Educational Welfare Officer was still the 'kid catcher' and when he caught Derek Bentley he whisked him before a magistrate. Briefly, on the recommendation of the authorities, although William Bentley says he arranged it, Bentley spent some time at an inferior school, at Ingram Road, Thornton Heath. A return to Norbury Manor, on Mr Bentley's insistence, was soon ended because

---

* Quoted in *To Encourage the Others* by David Yallop, London 1971

Bentley was misbehaving with a younger lad, supporting the comment of one of his teachers that the thirteen-year-old Bentley had a mental age of nine. He was back at Ingram Road by July 1947. By January 1948 he was back at Norbury Manor. As a teacher myself, I am well aware of what this nonsensical see-saw can do. Invariably it leads to failure and this was certainly so in the case of Bentley. One of his teachers summed the boy up in the way most of the world was to do after November 1952: 'A great lump of lard, an utterly worthless piece of humanity.'*

William Bentley, in *My Son's Execution*, glosses over the number of these changes of school.

In an effort to make life less miserable for his son (and it would be difficult to find a father who tried harder) he set up a workshop at the back of their home at 1, Fairview Road, where Derek could pursue his mechanical interests by tinkering with radios, televisions and bikes.

In March 1948 Bentley was in trouble with the law for the first time. He and another boy were charged at Croydon Juvenile Court with attempted shop-breaking and the theft of tickets and ten shillings from a bus conductor's till. Both were bound over for two years and once again, by magistrate's order, Bentley went back to Ingram Road, the ninth transfer since his schooling began.

In the summer of 1948 having left school, Bentley searched for work. William Bentley remembered the sheer joy on the boy's face after breakfast on his first day of maturity. He threw his arms around his mother's neck and said 'No school today!' Two weeks later, he was charged with another boy with stealing tools left lying around on a bomb site in Craignish Avenue, to the value of eighteen shillings. Reports, now lost to time, were prepared on Bentley's educational levels and he was sent to an approved school in Kingswood, Bristol.

A number of interesting points emerge from the period. First, the constable who brought Bentley home searched the house without a warrant. The police were to do this again on the night of November 2nd/3rd 1952. Technically, they didn't need one. But the offhand manner speaks volumes for the relationship between the men of Z Division and the working class public-at-large. Second, when brought before the magistrates he was asked – rather bizarrely, one might think – to spell the word 'fluorescent'. Not surprisingly, he could not.

* Quoted in *To Encourage the Others* by David Yallop, London 1971

William Bentley in recounting the tale spells it incorrectly too. If custody of delinquents were to be decided on such issues, the jails would be full and the streets empty. Third, ignoring Derek's being bound over earlier, William Bentley is outraged at the severity of the sentence. Fourth, according to William Bentley at least, the missing tools turned up . . .

At Kingswood it was discovered that Derek's IQ was 66 and his reading age 4½. This places him in the category of the feeble-minded or educationally subnormal, and in the brave new world of post-war society, where more stress was placed on these measurements than there would be today, this would, in other circumstances, have sentenced Bentley to a life of simple pleasures and relative poverty. That of course was not to be. David Yallop, in his book *To Encourage the Others*, points accusatory fingers in all directions, and finds Bentley's three-year sentence in Bristol 'another of the mysteries of the case'. Hardly a mystery. It was Bentley's second offence in six months and he had been bound over. There were those, perhaps, like Lord Goddard, who would have said he'd got off lightly.

By July 1950, a year ahead of schedule, Bentley was released from Kingswood, but technically remained under their long-distance – and therefore useless – supervision. A measure of the irrelevance of the school's views on Bentley is apparent from the Deputy Headmaster's letter to Bentley's father to 'see that he writes as often as possible to let us know how he is going on . . .' – and this of a boy who on 3 November 1952 could not spell his own name. For the last two years of his life, Derek Bentley was not well. His headaches worsened. He took phenobarbitone for them and became introverted and reclusive, for a year refusing to leave the house. It was his Uncle Albert, who now shared a room with him, who finally got the boy out, for a short walk on Streatham Common. Derek felt ashamed of his Approved School past – a shame that Christopher Craig was later to play on.

Thereafter for a time, things improved. He got a job as a furniture remover with Albert Hutchins, at Reeve's Corner. Hutchins knew his dad and Derek enjoyed the work. His first wage was £4. He gave £3 to his mother and the rest he spent on chocolates, cigarettes and flowers for the family. But he strained his back and had to give up by March 1952. It was while working for this firm that he bought himself a sheath knife to rip up upholstery. The knife was to assume a sinister aspect later. 'There was nothing sinister about it,' wrote William Bentley, 'Derek had no special liking for knives, or in fact any other weapons. He had certainly less than the normal healthy boy's attachment to them.'

His knife is now displayed in a glass case in Scotland Yard's Black Museum. As a toddler, Derek had preferred his sister's dolls to guns. And it was during that spring that he failed to qualify for National Service. The letter from the Ministry of Labour to William Bentley said:

When your son was medically examined on 11th February 1952, he brought with him a certificate from his doctor that he was subject to petit mal. The doctor who tested his mental capacity decided that he was mentally substandard and for these reasons he was placed in Grade IV.

Neither his epilepsy nor his mental capacity surprised the Bentley family. They felt throughout Derek's teens that they were living on a knife edge. A sudden accident, a blow, even a reversal of fortune, and the boy would withdraw into himself, with the constant threat of further fits.

Bentley's association with Craig dates from this period. It is a measure of Bentley's backwardness as much as Craig's dominance that it was Bentley who remembered the boy three years his junior from Norbury Manor School. William Bentley is adamant that his son did not know Craig from school (the assertion comes from Derek's garbled police statement) but I believe him to be wrong in this matter. One can imagine that a typical police question – which DCI Smith and DS Shepherd later denied posing – 'When did you first meet Christopher Craig?' would elicit an honest, if irrelevant, response such as this. It is a distinct pattern in the slow learner or retarded child to associate with younger children, because peer-group acceptance by their immediate contemporaries is usually denied them. Throughout the summer of 1952 a series of burglaries took place which may have been the work of the pair, and the Bentley parents in particular disapproved of Craig's influence. William Bentley even went to the police with the problem. But kindly old Sergeant Reed could not help because no specific crime had been committed. Derek himself got a job as a council dustman. ('Among our class,' said William Bentley defiantly, 'a dustman is not looked down on.') But he was demoted to road sweeper and finally lost the job entirely by July. More and more of his time now was spent in idleness. He tinkered a little with the radios and televisions in his father's repair shop. And he helped his mother with the housework, which he enjoyed very much.

The medical report on Derek Bentley made by Dr J. C. M. Matheson, Principal Medical Officer at Brixton Prison, on 5 December 1952 is illuminating more for what it tells us about the attitudes of Matheson and the system than about Bentley. The examination was certainly thorough. Matheson had read all the relevant reports, medical, educational and police, including the results of two electro-encephalograph tests carried out in 1949 and 1952. He had interviewed Bentley daily, had talked to his father, and had read the reports of officers who were in constant contact with Bentley from the time of his arrival following the hearing at Croydon Magistrates' Court on 3 November.

It is from this report that the evidence emerges of the mongol brother, younger than Derek, who died as an infant, and the fact, which seems to have come from William Bentley, that Derek was difficult to rear because of his bad temper. His early schooling shows a pattern of constant truancy and laziness, not helped by uncooperative parents. The social worker appointed to check on Derek after his release on licence from Kingswood found Derek's parents over-indulgent.

He associated with girlfriends – Iris's friend Rita was the subject of one such crush – but his usual companions were boys younger than himself. He was an occasional drinker and, like the rest of his family, a heavy smoker.

All in all, Matheson's report is hostile. We must remember that Bentley was accused of murder at this stage. All men are innocent until proven guilty. Unless of course they are dim kids from 'uncooperative' working-class backgrounds. To Matheson, Bentley had been allowed to grow up without any discipline or training. According to the Kingswood authorities, his father had encouraged an attitude of non-co-operation at variance with the letter the warden had written to Willian Bentley. His conduct at Brixton – 'Arrogant, boastful conversation' – made him unpopular with other inmates of the prison hospital.

Very little of this sounds like the real Derek Bentley. Unlike Matheson, I never met him. But I have got under the skin of the man over the last few months in a way that the Dr Mathesons of this world never can. Basically, Matheson's brief was to decide whether Derek Bentley was fit for the ordeal to come, rather like the regimental surgeon of the nineteenth century who examined a man before he was beaten with the cat o' nine tails. He decided he was.

> 'I am of the opinion that he is:
> (1) Sane;
> (2) Fit to plead to the indictment;
> (3) Fit to stand his trial.'

And that was where Matheson's job ended.

The real tragedy of Derek Bentley is not that he was epileptic; it is not that he was educationally subnormal; it is not that he was a casualty of war, shunted from school to school by an uncaring system; certainly not that he had a father who refused to believe his swan was a goose. The tragedy of Derek Bentley was that he met Christopher Craig.

Christopher Craig was born on the 19 May 1936, the youngest of nine children of a middle-class family. His father, Niven Craig, had been mentioned in dispatches while serving with the London Scottish Regiment in the Great War and had become a captain at the age of twenty-two. A respectable cashier (and banking was *the* mark of respectability pre- and post-war) in a large branch in Victoria Street, he commanded a Home Guard unit during World War Two. Ironically, his wife, sweet, caring and fond of poetry, had given a talk on the wireless on juvenile delinquency. Nearly all the Craig children had done well in their chosen careers. Mary was the eldest. She was thirty-two at the time of the case, married with two children. Jean, an ex-nurse, was also married, in her case with four children. Netta had two children and was married to a university lecturer. Bill was twenty-two, married with one child. Lita, at twenty, was engaged to a stockbroker's clerk; Lucy was a champion swimmer: '. . . a united family,' says Parris, 'free from any strain or disharmony which might be expected to produce delinquents.'

But it was the eldest and the youngest boy who dominated the headlines. Niven Craig junior was an exuberant lad whose energies were first diverted in wartime to stealing ammunition from a Home Guard store and attempting to row over to France to fight the Germans with one chum! The press of the day thought this laudable, as befitting the Dunkirk spirit. Nowadays, one suspects, Niven Craig would have been remanded for psychiatric reports. His army career was characterized by further thefts, while serving with the Gordon Highlanders. He stole no less than four jeeps and lorries travelling from Austria to Italy, by stopping their drivers with a revolver. He was placed in a military prison until 1950.

John Parris makes a great deal of Niven Craig in his book *Most of My Murders*. So does William Bentley in *My Son's Execution*. Certainly the most likely explanation of Christopher Craig's behaviour on the roof was his bitterness and bewilderment that the brother he idolized had become, as he saw it, a victim of the police. Parris says:

> Nevin [*sic*] was often away on mysterious expeditions from which he would return unexpectedly, sweeping up to the prosaic terraced house in Norbury in a huge American car. Invariably he would have a thick wad of notes carelessly rolled up in his pocket . . . [Christopher] began to emulate his brother in the flamboyance of his dress, and he came to think that there was only one way of escape from the boredom of ordinary routine and the menial occupation that was all an illiterate adolescent could hope for. He had dreamed once of being a brave soldier, as his father had been, but there were now no wars to fight, and it seemed to him that the only way to an adventurous life was to be against the law.

In September 1952 Niven Craig was arrested for the armed robbery he and others had committed back in March. In sentencing him to twelve years in prison days before the roof-top incident in Croydon, Mr Justice Hilbery said:

> You have, by your record, already shown that you are a young man determined to indulge in desperate crime. I have watched you carefully in the course of this trial and I can say that I do not remember, in the course of some seventeen years on the Bench trying various crimes of violence, a young man of your age [he was 26] who struck me as being so determined as you have impressed me as being . . . You are not only cold-blooded but from my observation of you I have not the least hesitation in saying I believe that you would shoot down, if you had the opportunity to do so, any police officer who was attempting to arrest you . . . I think you would do it absolutely coldly, utterly regardless of the pain you might inflict . . .*

* *Most of My Murders* by John Parris, London 1960

Lord Chief Justice Goddard was to deliver a similar tirade against Christopher Craig weeks later in the same court. If Parris and William Bentley are correct, then Christopher Craig could be proud of himself. He *had* emulated his brother in all respects.

But in Niven Craig at least there were signs of remorse. When he heard that Christopher had killed Sidney Miles, the older brother burst into tears and said to his sister, 'I've made him a killer. God! I'd do anything to get him out of this.' When Derek Bentley was executed, Niven Craig was found lying unconscious in his cell, his wrist slashed with glass from a broken window.

Throughout the trial, a picture was to emerge of Christopher Craig as a boy who had all the opportunities and threw them away. He went to good schools. He attended Bible classes at Streatham, but he too must have undergone the same sort of dislocation as Bentley. One hundred and forty flying bombs, remember, fell on Croydon during 1944–5. And Croydon was dangerously near Norbury, where the Craigs lived. There can be no doubt that Craig suffered in the same way as Bentley because of his dyslexia, then totally misunderstood and equated with stupidity. If a child, even a 'normal' one, cannot do something and is given no help or encouragement he simply switches off. That is, in effect, what Craig did. He accepted the alternative society's answer to the problem of reading – he looked at comics and films instead. But Craig had two outlets that Bentley had not – he was athletic, and this made him acceptable at school and to his friends; and he was verbally bright – witness his ripostes to Goddard and Humphreys at his trial.

On December 2 1952 he was given an electro-encephalograph examination at the Maudsley Hospital in Denmark Hill, not far from where he had been working as a mechanic at the Camberwell garage. From this and other tests carried out on him, it was fairly apparent that Christopher Craig was anything but a 'normal boy'. John Mays writes of juvenile delinquents in general: 'Most offenders are pathetic creatures, failures and misfits down on their luck and even in their truculent moods they are obviously inadequate personalities . . . Scratch the skin and find the baby!' And in prison, Mays contends, this situation gets worse – 'There go but ghosts of men that might have been!'

Sir David Henderson gave evidence to the Royal Commission on Capital Punishment. And Sir David was talking about the psychopath:

They may be adult in years, but emotionally they remain as dangerous children whose conduct may revert to a primitive, sub-human
level . . . They are in the most deplorable of all conditions, not sane
enough to be at large and not insane enough . . . to be suitable for
Bedlam.

Such a one was Christopher Craig. Irrational in his boyhood loathing
of the police, anti-authority, mean and vengeful, this boy hero-
worshipped the elder brother who was arrested with a loaded Luger
under his pillow and sentenced to twelve years for armed robbery
just three days before the roof-top incident. He was also the boy
who could exude charm when he wanted to and undoubtedly had the
sort of magnetic personality that drew to him silly grammar-school
boys like Norman Parsley and 'three-quarter-witted' ones like Derek
Bentley.

The same Dr Matheson who had reported on Bentley reported on
Craig from Brixton Prison on 3 December. There was a complication
here of course because of the boy's physical injuries after his fall from
the roof. He had arrived in Brixton on 11 November after his
appearance at Croydon Magistrates' Court where he had been helped
in by PC Pain. The source material that Matheson used was very
similar to that on Bentley. Craig's birth had been normal and his
mother reported that he was a good baby and easy to rear. No doubt
psychologists would have a field day with the fact that he wet his bed
until he was twelve. He was continually spoilt by his older brothers
and sisters, showed no inclination to work when he was at school and
truanted regularly. The only bright spot here was his swimming and
athletics.

His employments since leaving school had been brief. After two
weeks as assistant storekeeper with a firm of mechanics he 'left' after
being found in possession of a bunch of car keys. At the time of the
roof-top incident he was employed as a fitter in a garage where his
work was described as satisfactory and he earned £2 a week.

Craig gave Matheson the impression that he revelled in his situation.
He was self-satisfied and complacent, enjoying the limelight. The
doctor found him to be of average to below average intelligence, and
his dyslexia was due to lack of interest and application rather than
anything else. He was 'little interested' in the opposite sex and his
girlfriend (was this the 'Pam' he told the police to give his love to as he
jumped off the roof?) was a status symbol to make him feel 'grown up'.

Interestingly, because this image of bluff and swagger is very typical of the boy, he neither smoked nor drank.

Matheson concluded that Craig was very immature and unstable. He had little or no regard for others, even boasting of his ability to manipulate his family so that he got his own way. He was sane, he was fit to plead to the indictment and he was fit to stand his trial.

Somehow, although Matheson did not pull any punches with this report, its tone is far less censorious than that of Bentley. Perhaps it helped that Niven Matthews Craig was a bank official and a war hero. Perhaps some of Christopher's undeniable charm had rubbed off.

Bentley was introduced, or perhaps reintroduced, to Craig via Ron Hoare, a friend of the family, at the Christmas of 1951. According to Bentley, even before Craig knew his name he was boasting of the 'jobs' he'd pulled. 'I took an instant dislike to him,' wrote William Bentley, 'he struck me as impudent and shifty. There was this wild animal look in his eyes . . . There was nothing free and easy about this boy.'

On their second meeting, Lilian Bentley had expressed her fears about the boys' relationship. After all, twice before, Derek had been involved with someone else in shady goings on, and his father summed it up: '[Derek] was weak and easily led. He was not intelligent. His nature was soft and affectionate . . .'

Craig said, 'Surely you don't think I'd get him into trouble, Mrs Bentley?'

William Bentley was unnerved by the cruel, mocking tone of this fifteen-year-old and stunned by his self-assurance; 'I had felt the force of his personality and it had left a very unpleasant impression. Derek could never stand up to it . . . Compared with him, Derek was like water.'

What was the fatal attraction of one to the other? William and Lilian Bentley – although she mellowed later, feeling she had been unfair to Craig – tried to persuade Derek to jettison the bad influence. 'I just can't get rid of him, Dad . . . When I tell him to clear off, he just laughs.'

There was one occasion when William and Derek were polishing a car outside the house and Craig turned up.

'What a smashing car! What about lending it to me some time? There's a job I'd like to pull off, but I've got to have a car.'

Derek stepped over to Craig, threateningly:

'If you talk to my father like that I'll knock your block off. Clear out and don't come back.'

It wasn't until William also threatened to pin the boy's ears back that Craig actually left, however. When matters became worse and William made a move on a later occasion towards Craig, Derek looked terror-stricken, white and shaking and said: 'Don't, Dad! He'll get his gang to set about you if you paste him.'

Was that it? Was Derek Bentley simply afraid of Craig? The mention of the word 'gang' certainly ties in with the developing violent playground of South London. We've posed the question already – was the gang real? If it was the grammar-school boys Norman Parsley and Frank Fazey, then Mr Bentley had little to fear. But if it was the group who with Niven Craig carried out armed robbery in the March of 1952, then that was a different story.

I personally believe that the gang was largely a figment of Craig's twisted imagination – an imagination born of the cinema and the comic. William Bentley had summed it up: 'Compared with him, Derek was like water.' And Craig exerted his strange Svengali-like influence on others too, for example Fazey and Parsley. I believe that Craig and Bentley were a mutual appreciation society. Both flawed characters, both in their own ways, I suspect, unhappy, both dyslexic and below-standard educationally, they saw in each other a necessary companion. Craig because he had in Derek Bentley a stooge, a butt for his bravado and bluff, an audience for his swagger – and according to William Bentley at least, an accomplice for the enterprise he had in mind in early November 1952. And Bentley because he was easily overawed and easily impressed and easily led. He was delighted – as were his parents – when a 'college boy' like Norman Parsley came to call for him that fatal Sunday. Yet Norman Parsley too was an armed robber.

'They talk about haunted houses,' said William Bentley ruefully, '[Craig] haunted ours.'

Lilian Bentley came to believe – much to her husband's amazement – that they had misread Craig and that the best thing to do was to invite him in and ridicule his boasting. On the night of 1 November, however, an incident occurred which made her change her mind. Derek was at the cinema (he went once a week, normally to the Astoria, where Iris worked as an usherette) and Craig stood at the door, trying to impress nine-year-old Denis Bentley with his knuckle-duster, the one Lord Goddard was to play with later to such effect. He only succeeded in frightening the boy, who ran inside to tell his mother. When Mrs Bentley arrived, Craig proceeded to wave it around in what could only be described as a threatening manner. Trying her new tactic, she suggested he should put it away, as she felt sure the police would not approve of his carrying it.

'A fat lot I care for the police,' he told her, 'they're a lot of bloody fools. They'll never get me . . . We don't like the police, see! They've just given my brother Niven twelve years. Do you think I'm going to let them get away with that? I'm going to get my own back some day – and how! They'll never take me alive!'

Perhaps because he was hanged, perhaps because he was so patently innocent on that Croydon roof-top, most commentators on the case have concentrated on the life and crimes of Derek Bentley. It helps that his father wrote a book called *My Son's Execution* and that Craig's did not. But it is really Christopher Craig who is centre stage in this story. The whole crime hinges on him. His psychopathic nature, his hatred of authority in general and the police in particular, his uncontrollable urge to avenge his brother – 'Come on, you coppers. I'm Craig. You've just given my brother twelve years!' – it all adds up to endorse Lord Goddard's findings that he was 'one of the most dangerous young criminals who has ever stood in that dock.'

Take away the mother-fixation and replace it with brother-fixation; take away the machine gun (although the *Daily Mail* in the days after the roof-top claimed he carried and fired one); take away the Americanisms (although Craig himself adopted them), and you have public enemy number one James Cagney on that other roof-top in *White Heat*: 'Top of the world, Ma!'

The journalist Kenneth Allsop spent a week at the end of November 1952 with a typical Metropolitan Police division. He doesn't say which, as neither Craig nor Bentley had faced trial at that stage, but his reference to the district's having 'only a few days before . . . been upset by a markedly brutal and tragic incident', and the carelessly exposed initial 'Z' on the shoulder-tab of a constable in the photograph, make it quite clear that he is writing about Croydon. His title is 'Fear in the Suburbs' for the article he wrote for *Picture Post*, and the same issue is full of letters demanding a return to flogging for the 'cosh boys'. Allsop dubs 1952 'crime wave' year, but his statistics reveal that crime was actually *falling* in terms of robbery, with or without violence. When the overall figures are narrowed to Croydon – Allsop's 'one representative police division' – the wave becomes a mere ripple. A superintendent to whom he spoke nevertheless qualified all this by maintaining that the *level* of violence in violent crime was increasing markedly.

There was certainly a sense of ill ease in the area. A barmaid was typical of many when she said she would never feel safe until all policemen carried guns. Sales of padlocks, bolts and door chains rocketed. Ladies living alone began to carry pokers. Doors were answered after dark by residents who shone torches into callers' faces.

Allsop was at pains to put things in perspective: 'Until recently there has never been an incident involving revolvers – but it would be better sense if constables had considerably more firearms practice than the half hour they have had in the past three years . . . It is exceptionalness that causes it [the "cosh boy" furore] to be splashed in the newspapers. Even so, there is no room for complacency . . .' He concludes, rather limply, that 'Suburbia has not turned into another Soho.'

Tell that to the widow, Catherine Miles.

—— 3 ——

THE THIN BLUE LINE

> For it was that time in the shift when every policeman most dreads getting any sort of shout . . . half an hour to booking off time . . . The signal may be a sudden call on the radio . . . something you walk into without warning . . .

As I read Mike Seabrook's *Coppers*, dealing with his three years' experience in the Metropolitan Police in the early '70s, I was astonished how closely his description of the way he behaved during a traffic accident must have resembled the mental state of the policemen in the Craig and Bentley case, especially those on the roof-top:

> Of course, you know you're going to have to go in and your mind is already racing ahead, assessing what you are seeing, anticipating problems, making contingency plans, above all computing what must be done and whether you are going to make a mess of it when you do this or that . . . In a disciplined body and to a certain extent a fighting body, any member of which may have to go into violent action at any moment – each member knows that he depends on his colleagues utterly, perhaps for his very life.

I shall be accused no doubt of quoting out of context; of referring to a book written about a man's experiences twenty years after the event which is central to this book; of using as a yardstick the value judgements of a university graduate who faced a very different public and a very different set of problems from those encountered by the old Z Division in Fell Road, Croydon, in 1952. It is true that the image of the policeman has changed – and this chapter will discuss that image, because it is important. But in essence, Constable Seabrook's views are as relevant as those of Constables Harrison, McDonald, Jaggs, Pain and all the others in the Craig and Bentley case. They wore the same uniform, they faced the same fears, they had the same pride. It is this element of continuity which makes a 'disciplined . . . fighting body' like the Met the force it is.

What of the image of the police? Inevitably, and perhaps more so than with any other profession, the image comes not from fact, but from fiction. The early fictional policeman belongs first perhaps to the music-hall – he was the chubby, mustachioed buffoon, with big feet and a ruddy complexion, to whom you'd go to ask the time. The reality of this situation was that, in the nineteenth century, public clocks were still a rarity and pocket watches expensive. He was also caricatured in Gilbert and Sullivan's *The Pirates of Penzance*, where eager middle-class audiences were assured that his 'lot was not a happy one'. The country copper – not far removed from Enid Blyton's PC Plod – continued to enjoy or be annoyed by this characterization well beyond the First World War. The paintings of Lawson Wood from the 20's and 30's are archetypal of this sort of caricature. Most of them show elderly policemen with the build and rubicund face of a Botticelli angel terrorizing small boys in outsize cloth caps. His most famous, 'Nine Pints of the Law' – enjoying something of a vogue again in the Britain of the 80's – shows nine constables in full dress tunics and white gloves sitting on a bench downing steaming mugs of tea. Their collective age would seem to be about 540! The inference behind Wood's police paintings is that crime is not a problem (which may account for their popularity in the fear-stricken 80's) and that all the police have to do is to drink tea and feel the collars of naughty youngsters. It is unashamed nostalgia and none the worse perhaps for that.

An altogether more serious image – and a helpless one – emerged of the urban policeman by the turn of the century. Ahead of the field in satire then was *Punch*, which as *The London Charivari* had emerged to delight an early Victorian world in 1841. It was the Ripper case of 1888 and the inability of the Metropolitan and City forces to bring the murderer to justice which unleashed *Punch* against them. The plain-clothes men of Scotland Yard were referred to as 'the defective force' and the Queen herself was known not to be particularly amused by their shortcomings. What is especially interesting is that it is not until crime fiction arrives in force that the police come in for criticism in *Punch* at all. Search the volume for 1877, the year of the creation of the

CID, and there is scarcely a mention of the police. Peruse the pages of the 1901 volume and it is awash with broadsides. Why? Part of the reason must be the arrival in Baker Street of Sherlock Holmes, whose reputation and popularity are universal.

There is no such fan club for Sergeant Cuff, Inspector Lestrade, Chief Inspector Wexford or even Commander Dalgleish, coming from a century and a quarter of police fiction. Why is this? Basically, I suspect, when you've stripped away the element of flawed genius, the *frisson* caused by the cocaine addiction, the silly hat and the not-terribly-penetrating logic, you are left with the fact that Cuff, Lestrade, Wexford and Dalgleish are coppers. Holmes is not. The police are hidebound by convention, by report writing, by slow, orthodox methods. The nearer in time we come to the 80's, the less popular is the police image anyway, so Dalgleish arguably is less pleasant a character than Cuff, for instance. There is more romance, more excitement in being a private detective than in being a policeman. The reality has an interesting mirror. I have known several policemen in my time and they are all without exception average men. The only private detective I know is anything but average.

The image of the police in my boyhood in the 1950's must have been very different from that held by Craig and Bentley. A policeman was an honest man, upright, safe and from the vantage point of a five- or six-year-old, very, very big! There was, I suppose, an element of fear, but adults around me said there was nothing to fear. Policemen were nice men. It was undoubtedly television which underlined my view of the police. It was on television that I saw *The Blue Lamp*; and television's sequel to it, *Dixon of Dock Green*, was compulsory Saturday-night viewing for the family. More than anything else I think it was the friendly comforting face of old George Dixon, played by Jack Warner, with his 'Mind how you go', and his 'Look after dear old Mum' which strengthened the security I felt and made sense of the American conviction that our policemen were indeed wonderful.

More attractive than the uniformed beat copper who helped kids cross roads and lifted stranded kittens down from trees, was of course the detective. Again, television was for me the dominating influence. We did not own a set in time to watch *Fabian of the Yard*, but John Gregson's amiable Gideon, based on John Creasey's books, was exactly right in the 1960's. So was Raymond Francis's character, Inspector Lockhart, in *Murder Bag* which became *No Hiding Place* in 1959. Detectives wore trenchcoats and trilbies, they invariably smoked pipes, they spoke with immaculate public-school accents (all, I suspect, modelled on the film Gideon, Jack Hawkins) and they had the not-then-mannered habit of referring to the villain as 'Chummy'. Violence was almost non-existent, but when the time came a public-school right hook or a police manual armlock was enough to subdue the worst scoundrel.

Equally compelling was the series of black and white 'shorts', invariably juicy murder cases, introduced by Edgar Lustgarten and entitled *Scotland Yard*. Such was the lure of the programme that Norman Shaw's opera house which became New Scotland Yard in 1891, and was still in use as such in the 1950's, is *the* Yard; black Wolsley cars are *real* police cars and the most famous telephone number in the world is still Whitehall 1212.

The films of the late 50's, despite the reality of the fact that Bentley was dead and Craig was in prison, still maintained the fiction that detectives were nice ex-public-school boys – John Mills in *Tiger Bay*, Nigel Patrick in *Sapphire*, and Stanley Baker in *Violent Playground*. And that uniformed bobbies were essentially comic characters, like the team that rush around London in pursuit of *The Lavender Hill Mob*.

It was television once again that turned nasty. With Z Cars (1960 –78) there was a new realism. Policemen were faced, like the rest of mankind, with routine, with boredom. They worked unsocial hours and this wrecked marriages. Other than coppers they had no friends. And with the arrival of *The Sweeney* in the 70's, the bottom of the barrel had been reached. This, you could believe, was probably how Craig and Bentley saw the police – foul-mouthed, drunken, suspicious and decidedly working-class. They slept around, they swore and above all they were violent. John Thaw and Denis Waterman were a far cry from dear old Jack Warner.

The image of the policeman is important, because television fills our lives so totally. A large proportion of the viewing public probably has difficulty in distinguishing fiction from reality – Craig and Bentley with their comics almost certainly shared their problem. And reality has an uncanny knack of emulating fiction. As long ago as Arthur Conan Doyle, police discovered that faulty typewriters could indeed provide clues on cases, but it took the fictional Sherlock Holmes to point it out to them. A few years ago I spoke to a serving policeman who was in the Met in the 70's at the time when *The Sweeney* started. He told me that before that Metropolitan Policemen had a more or less conventional vocabulary. After it, they, in keeping with their television counterparts, 'got the wheels out', had 'the guv'nor on the blower' and occasionally carried 'shooters'. Even the police, it seemed, were losing hold on reality.

To most people, the image of the policeman is one obtained, then, from television, from films and from books; probably, at this less-than-literate end of the century, in that order. What of the reality?

The Metropolitan Police – Peel's 'Bloody Gang' – had been established in 1829 to meet another post-war period of rising crime. It had at first 3,000 officers, nearly all of whom were to be replaced either for drunkenness or bribe-taking during its first year. However unpopular the Peelers might be, however, they did reduce crime within the seventeen metropolitan districts and slowly people came to accept and even to trust them.

Z Division of the Metropolitan Police was created in 1921 as the suburbs grew and Greater London became even greater. Eight years later, Claude Pain became a constable in this division at a time when scandals galore were rocking this 'most public institution'. The papers were full of accusations against the Met of intimidation, wrongful arrest and perjury. Two examples will suffice. In April 1928, Leo Chiozza, better known as Leo Money, a well-known economist, was caught in a compromising situation with a Miss Irene Savidge on a Hyde Park bench. The park was notorious as a haunt for prostitutes and was then open all night. The case was thrown out at Marlborough Street Magistrates' Court, but Labour MPs in the Commons made an issue of it, claiming perjury (Miss Savidge made at least three contradictory statements) and even police brutality. A tribunal was set up and the relevant officers cleared, but such mud has a tendency to stick. Also in 1928, anonymous letters received at Scotland Yard implicated Sergeant Goddard (no relation, as far as I am aware, of the Lord Chief Justice) in the taking of bribes from Kate Meyrick who ran two notorious nightclubs, Proctor's in Gerrard Street and the Silver Slipper in Regent Street. Goddard, attached to what would nowadays be called the Vice Squad, earned £6 a week but owned a £2,000 house in Streatham and drove an expensive Chrysler car. In January 1929, Goddard was found guilty, fined £2,000 with costs and sentenced to eighteen months' hard labour. Sadly, it was part of that lingering tradition which has never left the police in general and the Met in particular. From the 'trial of the detectives', Druscovitch, Palmer and the others, in 1877, to the planting of evidence on innocent students by Challenor in the 1960's, the taint is a continuing tradition. And tradition is a vital ingredient to the police force. Without it, the institution cannot be properly understood. 'The police society,' wrote Seabrook in 1987, 'has a very long collective memory. Officers talk about the police strike of 1919 as if it is a personal memory, though most of their fathers were unborn when that strike took place.'

The policeman's lot in the 1930s, however, improved quite considerably. Claude Pain remembers his first nights on the beat when the crusty old copper who was his 'parent', in modern police phraseology, showed him how to hook his belt around park railings and so get a good night's sleep. Such procedures, of course, were not to be found in any training manual, and such procedures, which must have been widespread among the older constables, call into question Lord Birkenhead's words at the end of the Savidge affair: 'There is no finer, no more honourable, no more honest and no more courageous force of men in the world.'*

The beat of the Metropolitan constable had been defined by Commissioner Mayne in 1829 as an area which could be covered in fifteen or twenty minutes at a steady pace of 2½ miles per hour. The monotony of this is indescribable – and despite Commissioner Byng's reorganization of beats to confuse criminals and refresh constables, it is essentially a dull, routine part of the job. So the fixed point system which Dickens knew, of constables reporting at an agreed place and time, disappeared during the 30's to be replaced by telephone boxes and foot patrols linked to cycle and motor units. An Information Room was set up at Scotland Yard to liaise by wireless with the nucleus of vehicles that was to become, in the fullness of time, the Flying Squad.

David Ascoli says of the Met at this time: 'It remained an ultra conservative, artisan institution, still wedded to a hierarchical structure . . . The police service, with its lack of incentives, still attracted brawn rather than brains.'

It is the Metropolitan Police Force in the post-war period which interests us most. Ascoli says of this age of austerity: 'The new society, with its vision of a synthetic Utopia, its appeal to materialism, its tolerance of indiscipline and its politics of envy, has much to answer for . . .'

* Quoted in *The Queen's Peace* by David Ascoli, London 1979

To Ascoli – and to playwrights like John Osborne – it was the age of angry young men. Angry young men like Christopher Craig. Ascoli paints a particularly grim picture of London itself: 'Indeed, London in the post-war period had much in common with Rome in the years before the fall of the Western Empire; a city stifled by bureaucracy, decadent, corrupt, happily feasting on borrowed bread and circuses, its churches empty.' And he continues his attack in a different direction when he calls into question the now dubious phrase of Prime Minister Harold Macmillan, 'You've never had it so good': 'There are very few Metropolitan policemen of the post-war period who would not find that a more offensive – and provocative – commentary on the temper of our times than all the radical invitations to public indiscipline put together . . .'

For this was the era of Neville Heath, the brutal sadist who murdered Margery Gardner in June 1946; of John Haigh who almost succeeded in dissolving Mrs Durand Deacon in a tub of acid in February 1949; of John Christie, whose house and garden at 10, Rillington Place were found littered with asphyxiated corpses early in 1953. And of course, this was the era of the violent playground, where firearms became more common, and among the police casualties of those firearms were Nathaniel Edgar and Sidney Miles.

The death of Sidney Miles is of course central to this book. PC Edgar, patrolling in plain clothes in Southgate, North London, was shot three times on 13 February 1948 by a felon suspected of a series of burglaries in the area. Before dying, he was able to tell colleagues that his assailant was Donald Thomas, who was duly found guilty at the Old Bailey in April of that year and sentenced to death. His arrest was very similar to that of Niven Craig, again for robbery, four years later. Thomas too had a loaded Luger under his pillow. Unlike Bentley, Thomas was lucky. The death penalty was under temporary suspension at the time and he was given life imprisonment, being released on licence in April 1962.

The new government was a socialist one. One of its leading lights was Aneurin Bevan, the man who had branded the Police College at Hendon a Fascist institution some years earlier. The government of Clem Attlee valued its policemen about as much as that of Margaret Thatcher values its teachers today. So the police were low on the government's rate of priorities and in post-war reconstruction and rationing and rehousing there were bigger, more urgent problems. Even so, changes and reforms did take place. A milestone occurred of itself when Sir Harold Scott was appointed Commissioner of the Police of the Metropolis in June 1945. He was the first man for a very long time to hold this post who did not come from the narrow, blinkered services. Under him, the Police Act of 1946 increased pay, but it was a pittance and differentials with other walks of life were all too obvious. A further 47 square miles were added to the Metropolitan area and the bombs had caused a chronic shortage of accommodation for the men. In the year of the Craig and Bentley case, 1,487 of them had no official quarters at all. The poor pay and conditions did not attract back into the force those who had left it for other services. In what Ascoli calls the 'new world of the five-day week', police shifts had little appeal. In May 1948 a constable's basic pay stood at £5. 5s. per week and the Oaksey Committee established in that month recommended pay increases by 1949 to £340 per year (salary had a more professional status than that of the working-class weekly wage). This was to rise to £420 after 22 years' service. Claude Pain had two years to serve to achieve this goal when the Oaksey Report was published.

And in terms of the increased violence, the authorities did not help in toying with the abolition of the death penalty. In the late 40's and 50's, condemned man after condemned man received a reprieve – the Home Secretary's motor cycle dispatch rider arriving at the prison gate. Ascoli quotes a Met sergeant at the time who said, 'I think that villains almost felt sorry for the police.'

The debate on capital punishment in Parliament in 1948 had produced two camps, bitterly divided. And it had rapidly become a party matter. Broadly, Labour and many Liberals stood behind the Labour Home Secretary, Chuter Ede, in demanding an end to the ghastly process. Conservatives stood behind Lord Goddard of the 'flog 'em and hang 'em' school and took naïve comfort from Sir John Anderson of the Home Office, who assured the House that not one innocent man had been hanged since 1900.

In physical terms the appearance of the police force was altered. Lawson Wood's Victorian policeman of the 30's with long coat and high stand collar disappeared, to be replaced by an altogether younger man with open-necked tunic, shirt and tie, lightweight versions of which were available for the summer. Not long into the future, the increasing use of the cars would see the increasing use of the flat peaked cap with its distinctive check headband and even, something which would have horrified former Commissioners like Byng, Trenchard and Game, policemen patrolling in their shirtsleeves – and in the company of policewomen!

In 1951 Scott's changes went further. Borrowing ideas from the strangely more enlightened Aberdeen force, 'team' policing became the order of the day. Six constables under a sergeant linked to the Information Room via a two-way radio car established what is still the operational tactic of the Met as far as crime prevention is concerned. And in the same year, a Police Cadet Corps was established. Within a fortnight, there were over one thousand applicants (Claude Pain's son Ray was one of them) and 175 of these were trained at Hendon and posted to divisions prior to their National Service.

Sir Harold Scott was still Commissioner at the time of the Craig and Bentley case and the papers carried his photograph shaking hands with the Croydon roof-top policemen. He resigned in August 1953, to be re-placed by Sir John Knott-Bower whose father had been Commissioner of the City of London Force during the Siege of Sidney Street – that other famous shootout – in 1911. Sir David Maxwell Fyfe, the Home Secretary who appointed him, was as exasperated by him as most other people were. David Ascoli quotes a superintendent's comment on Knott-Bower: 'He was a nice man when what we needed was a bit of a bastard.'

By the May of 1955, when Derek Bentley had been dead for two and a half years, *The Times* threw up its hands in despair and declared 'The British people, in their attitude to civilized standards, are fast becoming ungovernable.'

The Criminal Investigation Department was altogether a different matter. Born out of the small and unsung Detective Branch at the Old Scotland Yard behind Whitehall Place in 1843, it was largely the creation of an extraordinary if arrogant young lawyer, Howard Vincent. The year 1877 saw the trial of the detectives in which a number of Yard men were convicted of taking bribes. The reputation of the Branch was in ruins, but Vincent produced a paper which he submitted to the Home Secretary, offering to salvage what was left and to reorganize on the lines of the Parisian Sûreté, of which he had first-hand knowledge. Given the quirky nature of nineteenth-century policing, the Home Secretary agreed and gave Vincent the job of carrying it out. Soon after its inception the CID lost Vincent for good. His was too fertile a mind and his spirit too restless to stay with his creation and thereafter a third Assistant Commissioner was created to run the CID. Given that its purpose was essentially detection rather than prevention of crime, that its officers wore plain clothes rather than uniform and that by and large it attracted men of superior brain power, a large and widening gulf was perhaps inevitable between them and the rank and file copper of the uniformed branch. Ascoli says:

> From then on [1878] the CID had become in effect a separate police institution, divorced from the uniform branch and treated by successive commissioners ... as a privileged élite, whose plain clothes could cover, in the interests of crime detection, a multitude of sins ... It is beyond argument that by the summer of 1922 the CID had become a thoroughly venal private army.

Commissioner Trenchard had been all too aware of this problem, as he wrote in 1934:

> ... the state of jealous rivalry ... which has so long existed between the CID and the uniformed branch is gradually being put to an end and the two branches integrated into one harmonious whole.

In that he couldn't have been more wrong. There is a tendency to assume, at least in the literature that I have read and the people I have talked to, that if police corruption exists anywhere – and it does – then it exists largely in the CID. So Ascoli writes of Trenchard's inability to curb his detectives: 'The man who could talk with kings seemed frightened of corrupt constables.' And Seabrook says: 'Now it is well enough established that there are bent policemen ... and for the CID in particular, the opportunities are tempting in the extreme.' And of the greatest relevance of all, Claude Pain told me: 'There were some funny things going on in those days. If seven or eight superior officers tell you something, you start to believe it.'

What happened on that Croydon roof-top that wet Sunday night thirty-seven years ago has a great deal to do with the relationship between uniformed men and the CID.

We have looked in this chapter at the institution which gave *raison d'être* to Fairfax, McDonald, Harrison, Jaggs and the others involved, as in the last chapter we looked at the situation which created

Craig and Bentley. It is important that we understand both sides in the conflict, particularly the pressures that both sides faced. As I have been writing this chapter, staring up at me from the newspaper cutting on my desk has been the face of the present Commissioner of the Police of the Metropolis, Sir Peter Imbert. In an article by Barbara Jones in the *Daily Mail* in the summer of 1988, Imbert was quoted as being worried that his officers were writing and publishing their memoirs without consulting him first. The particular instance was occasioned by a series of articles in the press by ex-Detective Chief Superintendent Drummond Marvin, who 'revealed the secrets of police work' concerning the prosecution for indecency of MP Harvey Proctor and the death of television personality Russell Harty. Imbert sent a letter to all divisions making it quite clear that he would take proceedings under the Official Secrets Act against any officer who went into print without his written authority. As the *Daily Mail* pointed out, it is rather unfortunate that Imbert's immediate predecessors – Commissioners Mark, McNee and Newman – have all published their memoirs. Mark's book in particular, *In the Office of Constable*, is a milestone in the story of police and, like Seabrook's *Coppers*, ought to be compulsory reading for anyone interested in the maintenance of law and order.

But it is more unfortunate that in the decade in which the police have become 'filth', 'pigs' and 'scum', the decade in which Constable Keith Blakelock could be hacked to death by a mixed-racial mob in Brixton, the decade in which the police need all the help they can get, the Commissioner of the Metropolitan Police should imply that just possibly, some of his officers have something to hide.

Constable Claude Raymond Pain was a copper of the old school. When I met him in the summer of 1988 he stood clearly over six foot, had the firm handshake and steady gaze of a man who had spent his working life as the island of calm in umpteen seas of hysteria. He is eighty years old, but his judgement is sound and his memory is long. Only his conscience is bothering him a bit . . .

He had joined the Metropolitan Police in 1929, the year of its centenary which the 'most public institution in the world' celebrated five months too early. His first posting was in fact to J Division and he has in his possession a studio photograph taken during his first year in the force. He sits smiling in a still Victorian-looking tunic with its white-metal buttons, whistle chain and stand collar bearing his rank number, 330J. One of his first nights of duty when he joined H Division was at the end of November 1936, when he helped tackle the fire that burnt down the Crystal Palace. In many ways it was the end of an era. As PC 241Z he was remembered for many years in Selsdon and Croydon as a gentleman, archetypally the 'nice' policeman; as far as it is possible to be in the real world, George Dixon.

At the outbreak of war, the force was, as was the norm, under-strength, at that time by 930 men. Massive bombing raids were expected, after the appalling experience of the Spanish town of Guernica. Numbers were therefore vital and they were found by creating three reserve forces. The first was composed of pensioners, men in their fifties and sixties, who re-enlisted. The second was filled with Specials, who had enlisted on a full time basis. And the third, the official Police War Reserve, were to serve for the duration only. This gave the force a new total strength of 45,413, but the bombers didn't come and the 'Phoney War' gave the Met a chance to prepare and even the complacency to reduce numbers. By the beginning of 1942 men under thirty were at liberty to join the armed forces proper. The war years were full and hectic and the men of the police of the metropolis responded admirably. Security became a national obsession. In a country where careless talk could cost lives and where a secret fifth column was thought to be operating, pigeon fanciers, kite fliers and throwers around of fireworks were watched very carefully. The first bomb fell on the borough of Addington, not far from Croydon, on 19 June 1940 as part of the Luftwaffe's daylight raids on airfields. On Saturday, 7 September, the night-time blitz to sap civilian morale began. In the first phase of this Battle of Britain, between September 1940 and July 1941, there were 1,000 alerts, 23,000 deaths and over 40,000 injuries, among them a little boy called Derek Bentley.

On 11 May 1941 there was a direct hit on Scotland Yard itself. And in 1944 and '45, 2,341 flying bombs fell on the Metropolitan district, killing 7,988 and injuring 20,783. Despite all this or probably because of it, the morale of the force was never higher. Crime figures dropped. The force won 276 honours and awards for gallantry, including 82 George Medals. Even the animals were not forgotten – three police horses were given the Dickin medal for bravery! Yet by the end of the war when Philip Game resigned as Commissioner, the force stood at only 12,231 men and women, its lowest figure for over sixty years.

During the war, Pain had a living-out beat in Selsdon where he was the local bobby to hundreds of people. Post-war generations have lost touch entirely with this image and the 1980's, interestingly, have seen countless demands for a return of this role. Scrap the patrol cars and put more men back on the beat. There is perhaps no substitute in terms of mutual understanding for the 2½ m.p.h. foot patrol. Long before the advent of 'lollipop' men and women to ease pressure on the uniformed branch, one of Pain's duties was to supervise the crossings of pupils at Selsdon Secondary School. His family had been evacuated to Wales. Mrs Anne Pain was born in Merthyr Tydfil and even now, after years in South London, has a trace of the old accent. She spent most of the war packing parachutes at the Arsenal at Bridgend. Pain's duties also involved work on crashed aircraft. Because of the proximity of Croydon airport and the Luftwaffe's attempts to smash the morale of London in 1940 and again via the 'doodlebugs' in 1944–5, Pain's beat was in the front line. In the dogfights of 1940 he had a great deal to do with the RAF. He was cycling along Featherbed Lane in Shirley one day when a Spitfire in trouble, trailing black smoke, crashed into a garden in Hartland. Pain pedalled off in the direction of the descending parachute, but the young pilot was dead before he hit the ground. And in war, accidents add to the casualties. Pain saw two aircraft taking off from Biggin Hill collide with each other over the trees at Kingswood. They still haven't found all the wreckage.

After the war Pain took up dog handling. He was to become No. 1 Dog Handler at Croydon after the Craig and Bentley incident. And commendations flowed from the Bench, as when he and Sidney Miles chased a housebreaker half-way across London by bus!

Claude Pain retired from the Metropolitan Police Force on 11 November 1954, two years and nine days after the roof-top incident in Croydon. He was of course still a relatively young man and able to take up employment. For a while he worked as a surveyor for Croydon council and in 1957 took a step far less common then than now – he emigrated with his family to California and got a job in security in St Luke's Hospital, Pasadena. It does not seem to have been a success, for in 1958 the Pains returned and Claude worked as a caretaker for the council for the next sixteen years. He retired at sixty-seven but grew bored sitting at home and worked in a local hardware shop until he was seventy-five. He is content now to stay at home with his wife and his cat and receive regular visits from children and a horde of grandchildren who climb all over him – 'I don't know who half of them are!' he told me with a grin.

Only his conscience is bothering him a bit . . .

When I began to write this book and it began to take shape, I thought that this would be the easiest chapter of all, but in fact it has proved the most difficult. Difficult because of the paucity of information. I believed – and still believe – that we can only know the truth of what happened on that Croydon roof-top if we have profiles of all the participants. Thanks to his father, we know most about Derek Bentley. We know rather less about Christopher Craig.

And of the policemen, what? I had assumed in my innocence that service records of all those involved would be available to the public, but apparently, the same regulations apply here as in the Craig and Bentley case itself. Only if the men concerned choose to talk to me can I gain firsthand information about the case, their part in it or indeed anything about their careers. Apart from Pain, then, we are left to the notoriously ill-informed views of the newspapers.

Sidney Miles comes to us through the haze of eulogy. His death and the brutal manner of it shocked Croydon and the nation in 1952, and although the terms of respect and honour are no doubt due to him and are certainly understandable, they are in the end empty rhetoric. Witness the example of the Archdeacon of Croydon, a man who did not know Miles at all: 'PC Miles was typical of what we and the world have come to expect and find in the unrivalled police force of this land.'

The *Croydon Times*, more likely perhaps to get the feel of the situation than the nationals, quoted a senior officer at Croydon police station: 'He was a man who was absolutely fearless. The courageous part he played in last Sunday's shooting affray was typical of him.'

Miles had been appointed driver of a wireless car where speed, instinct and guts were the order of the day. He was born at Eastry, near Sandwich in Kent, and worked as a gardener before joining the Metropolitan Police, a few months after Claude Pain. His career was very similar to that of Pain. They were friends and shared one citation when they gave chase to crooks in the high-speed bus chase mentioned above. Miles was commended three times for gallantry in effecting arrests, the last in 1941, and his proficiency in first aid was vitally important in his role in air raids. He was a keen sportsman, playing football and cricket for Croydon Police Athletic Club. He lived with his wife, Catherine, at Tower View, Shirley, and they had no children. At the time of his death he was forty-two years old.

The *Croydon Advertiser* was more forthcoming. Sir Harold Scott, then Commissioner of the Met, visited Croydon Police Station on

Wednesday, 5 November 1952, to express his sympathy to relatives, friends and colleagues of the dead man. An unnamed colleague described Miles as 'a good type and a good, efficient officer. Until a few years ago, he was an immaculate football full back', and was said never to have fouled a man on a pitch in his life. Another colleague said of his cricket that he was 'always good for knocking sixes'. He had served with the Royal Army Medical Corps (hence his proficiency in first aid) between 1926 and 1929. He held the police long service medal (as did Pain) and in 1935 was commended by the Commissioner for zealous and efficient conduct.

Archdeacon Tonks said at the funeral service:

On a quiet Sunday night, we lost one who we could ill afford to lose.

It is, first and foremost, to pay a tribute to him and his devotion to duty and through him to the whole police force, that this great representative congregation has assembled.

Sidney Miles served in that force for twenty-two years. He lived an exemplary life within it and as a private citizen. He was one who performed his duties, whatever they were, promptly, fearlessly, courteously, with fairmindedness and in an even temper. He had that quiet courage which prompted him to tackle the difficult and even dangerous task without thought of self, with no hesitation or delay and to carry it through without ostentation or self-seeking. He was an excellent member of a team, a man whom others were glad to have at their side in a critical situation.

Miles's brother, from Rochester, was also in the police, as a Special Constable. He walked with Catherine Miles behind the flag-draped coffin with the dead man's helmet, ceremonial belt and the wreath of red carnations, white chrysanthemums and violets from his wife. His allotment would go untended.

'Sidney Miles was the finest type of policeman you could wish to meet,' said another colleague at Fell Road. 'In our words he was a man with a ton of guts. He had a terrific energy in tackling any and every kind of job. There was no particle of fear in his body. Sidney had a long time in the force. It's true he hadn't had promotion, but as a man on the beat he had given first-class service. Everyone liked him.'

So the popular, unassuming, unambitious constable must step back into the yellowed pages of history. Ironically, he shouldn't have been on the roof-top at all. Typical of the man, he had swapped duties at the last minute to help a colleague. In the absence of official Metropolitan documentation, that is all there is.

'He hadn't had promotion . . .' and I suspect, like Claude Pain, he didn't want any. Thank God for such Indians. What of the would-be Chiefs?

The senior man on the roof-top was Frederick Fairfax. In most of the photographs I have seen of him, he is smiling; in the contemporary newspapers, the sling is very prominent. And why not? It made good copy. Fairfax was a hero and he knew it. In the helter-skelter pace of history, especially post-war history, no one is remembered for very long. But the narrow eyes have a certain hardness and there are those who do not remember him with fondness.

Ray Pain was sixteen at the time of the Craig and Bentley case. He was a police cadet. He was to go on to become a military policeman in the army and to face the bullets of Eoka terrorists in Cyprus. No stranger to physical courage himself, he admits being terrified of Fairfax.

Again, national papers let us down. The *Daily Express* for Monday 3 November 1952, gets Fairfax's age right (37) but proceeds to refer to him as PC, and claims that he travelled to Tamworth Road in the same car as Sidney Miles.

The *Croydon Advertiser* comes to the rescue. Fairfax had been at Croydon for nearly six years. He is referred to as a 'wartime commando captain' and 'is known for his unassuming manner and his quiet efficiency in the CID branch of Croydon'. According to Ray Pain, who knew all his father's colleagues, often making tea for them on duty, Fairfax ruled Fell Road station with a rod of iron. Fairfax's immediate superior, DCI John Smith, sang his praises to local reporters:

> He is a well trained police officer, a pretty good boxer and generally knows how to look after himself. But that doesn't count when you're facing bullets . . . a man who faces bullets from that [the sawn off Eley revolver] with a wound in his shoulder, as Fairfax did, is a remarkably brave man. No effort should be spared in paying tribute to him.

Fairfax joined the Met in 1936 and was married with one son. He was frequently to be seen acting as a qualified ABA judge in amateur boxing contests in and around Croydon and, like Miles and Pain, had an exemplary record as a police officer. He had been commended six times for gallantry in arresting housebreakers and shopbreakers. His hobby, like that of Derek Bentley, was mechanics.

Fairfax handled himself tolerably well at the trial but his perform-ance there and his involvement on the roof will be discussed in greater detail later. All the papers at the time sang his praises as one would expect. Virtually all David Yallop's comments on him refer directly to the case in hand and although he interviewed Fairfax, we are no closer to the kind of man Fairfax was then or has since become. Similarly Fenton Bresler interviewed Fairfax for his biography of Lord Goddard and again was only concerned with the immediacy of the case itself.

Mrs Beecher-Brigden told me that her husband – the nebulous 'PC Bugden' of Yallop's book – thought highly of Fairfax. For a while on his retirement, following his receipt of the George Cross and pro-motion to Detective Sergeant First Class, Fairfax seems to have run a shop, but it wasn't successful. As one ex-policeman told me, 'People knew him for what he was and no one would go in there.' He set up a private enquiry agency but by virtue of the confidential nature of this kind of work, I have no idea how successful that was. He now lives near Yeovil in Somerset and has refused to co-operate in any way with this book.

Another policeman earnest for notice and promotion was Norman Harrison. In most of the contemporary photographs he is seen smiling, clean-cut, blond-haired, fresh-faced. I was lucky enough to find another source *re* Harrison since the newspapers, apart from carrying his photograph and name, are unforthcoming. The other source is a former police officer who knew Harrison in the years after the case. As fellow sergeants (Harrison got his promotion shortly after Fairfax) my informant got to know him quite well. He remembers a friendly, thoroughly nice individual, conscientious and a 'good, honest copper'. Harrison never mentioned the Craig and Bentley case and my infor-mant had the sensitivity never to ask. Harrison too had faced Craig's bullets; he had seen Sidney Miles die in front of him. They are not experiences that men like to share. Harrison too has refused his co-operation with this book.

James McDonald died in hospital on 13 December 1988. And there, as far as further research is concerned, all lines of enquiry end. Of all the policemen at the trial, McDonald seemed least comfortable with his evidence. And of all the policemen at the trial, he is the only one other than DS Shepherd who is seen in another incident in the local

Croydon newspapers. On 23 October 1952 he was the wireless operator in a patrol car driven by PC D. Day who apprehended three men attempting to break into a wine merchant's. In the chase that followed, both cars reached seventy miles an hour until the villains' shooting brake hit two walls and collided with an iron post in Drummond Road, North End. Day and McDonald gave chase on foot once the thieves had tumbled out of their vehicle and McDonald threw his torch at one of them, Frederick Miller, who staggered and was subsequently arrested. It was simply another routine call. Another quiet autumn night. McDonald, too, slips quietly away from the researcher's net.

The last policeman on the roof was Robert Jaggs. Older than Harrison, with badly fitting teeth and a shock of dark wavy hair, he appears in none of the contemporary papers I have seen, except as a name. The informant who knew Harrison also knew Jaggs, but not so well. Jaggs ended his career as a constable and my informant knew him in a supervisory capacity. He remembers having no call for criticism, but other than that, cannot in fairness assess the man at all. Bob Jaggs was found dead in a South London street in 1978.

'The rest is silence.' What was to be a straightforward review of the careers of five policemen up to the night of 2 November 1952 has become nothing of the sort. The next page you see will be blank as a token of the vast amount of material which lies hidden. Hidden because it is the system. Hidden because it is in somebody's interests to keep it hidden. Hidden in Yallop's phrase because there is a need to bolster up the police force of this country – 'to encourage the others'.

—— 4 ——

TORTURE BY HOPE

Derek William Bentley, you are nineteen years of age; it is my duty to pass upon you the only sentence which the law can pass for the crime of wilful murder. The sentence of the Court upon you is that you be taken from this place to a lawful prison, and there to a place of execution, and there you suffer death by hanging, and that your body be buried within the precincts of the prison in which you shall have been last confined before your execution; and may the Lord have mercy on your soul. Take him down.*

And they took Derek Bentley down. As they had from the Croydon roof-top. As they were to do from the gallows.

It was Thursday, December 11 1952. The 'trial of the century' was over. William Bentley watched his son go. He sensed someone squeeze his arm in sympathy and sat, uncomprehending, while Goddard removed the black cap from his wig and passed sentence on Christopher Craig. Lilian and Iris were in a cafe across the road from the Bailey, unable to bear the tension of the hour. Bentley didn't wait to hear Goddard praise the men of Z Division. Crying inwardly, he found his way to the outer doors, then across the street on that cold, foggy morning.

It was their eyes he couldn't bear. They sat, still in their coats with empty teacups in front of them, looking at him, pleading silently for everything to be all right. It would be a prison sentence, wouldn't it? A few years at worst. Derek had done nothing. He hadn't shot anybody. He was under arrest at the time. Fairfax had said so. So had the Prosecution.

'Well, Will?' Lilian broke the silence between them.

* *Notable British Trials* op. cit.

[83]

Bentley had had perhaps five minutes to compose the words. He must get it right. He mustn't give way now.

'They've found him guilty,' he said, 'but it will be all right. The jury have recommended him to mercy.'

Lilian and Iris broke down, collapsing into each other's arms. Little Denis, his truculent face buried for a moment in his mother's sleeve, looked up – 'Is it bad, Dad?'

What do you tell a nine-year-old kid? That a man is going to hang his brother? And wasn't it a nine-year-old kid, little Pearl Ware, who'd started the whole thing in the first place?

'Not so bad, son,' Bentley ruffled his boy's curly hair. 'It might be worse.'

But not in his wildest dreams could William Bentley imagine how.

Somehow, they all got home. Bentley put his women to bed and called the doctor who brought sedatives. They were once a family. They were still a family. But for now William would have to do all the thinking, all the planning. He had a sharp mind, he was nobody's fool, but in the weeks and years ahead, he was to go through the mangle of fighting the State, with its centuries of tradition and power and disregard for the common man. And the first stage of his plan, the first step into the arena, was to see Derek in the condemned cell at Wandsworth.

Wandsworth Prison had been built in 1851 as part of the programme of prison building and reform which began with Pentonville and Peel's Gaols Act. Behind its grim grey façade, the Bentleys visited their eldest son in surroundings very different from those in Brixton. Two cells were converted into a single room for the purpose of interview, divided by a glass partition up to eye level. Voices carried through an iron grille near the floor, giving them a muted, deadened effect. There was to be no touching. None of them would ever hold Derek again.

It took three or four of these daily visits for an air of normality to descend. The brittle cheerfulness, the strained smiles, the sudden hysterical laughter for no reason at all, gave way to calm and a grim determination for the fight ahead. Derek's thoughts, at that first meeting and subsequently, turned to the widow, Catherine Miles. He wanted his father to contact her, to tell her how sorry he was. He had heard that she didn't believe he ought to die for what had happened. How easily the word tripped off the tongue – 'I'm not going to die, of course,' he was quick to assure his family.

[84]

His family did their best. They called personally on Mrs Miles, but someone else opened the door with a message that, given the difficulty and pain of the moment, she could not face them. They understood. Perhaps they had been wrong to call. But for Derek's sake they had to. To let her know how grateful they were. In the book he wrote four years later, William Bentley said: 'But to Mrs Miles goes the honour of rising above a deep personal sorrow to express the opinion that Derek should not die.'

Christmas came and went. The saddest Christmas the Bentleys had known or were to know. What kept them going, in those awful daily visits to Wandsworth, was Derek's own strength and determination. He spoke naturally of his plans, yet they were plans based on a misunderstanding and an irrational hope pinned on the Appeal set for 13 January. Even if all went well, the Appeal was not likely to set Derek Bentley free, to be with his family. Perhaps he knew it. Perhaps they knew it. But no one said it. Such things were not to be spoken.

On Christmas Eve they had heard the laughter of the prisoners and the warders. Derek had joined in, telling his dad how they'd given him the best cell in the place, with its own bath. A generation of prison officers has come and gone since the abolition of the death penalty. God knows what it was that kept such men cheerful, spending day and night with a man about to die. Mistakenly, on Christmas Day, the Bentleys presumed too much on the good nature of these men. They bought a basket of fruit for Derek as a present, to be told that he could not accept it. It was contrary to prison regulations. They took it home. And there it stayed, withering like the family's hope, until after his execution.

The Court of Criminal Appeal dates from 1907. Its purpose is to review a decision made by an inferior court in the instance of a guilty verdict. Such appeals were standard practice in the days of capital punishment. Accordingly, on 13 January 1953, this court met to debate the case of Derek Bentley, before a panel of three judges: Mr Justice Croom-Johnson, presiding, Mr Justice Ormerod and Mr Justice Pearson. William Bentley, as it might be you or I, would have gone to that Appeal armed with rationalism, with the same common sense that Lord Goddard had claimed to have brought to the trial itself. The common sense that said that Derek Bentley had not fired a shot. He had not carried a gun. He had offered no resistance to arrest and he was technically under arrest at the time of the shooting of Sidney Miles. But common sense, whatever Goddard's misappropriation of the term, had little place in the British judiciary of 1953. Frank Cassels, representing young Bentley now as he had at the trial, could only appeal in terms of law.

And his appeal was twofold. Firstly, that Goddard in his summing up to the jury, had not put Bentley's case either fairly or at sufficient length. The trial itself will be dissected in a later chapter, but Goddard's reference to Bentley's position ran to a mere five lines:

> In the case of Bentley, Bentley's defence is: 'I didn't know he [Craig] had a gun, and I deny that I said: "Let him have it, Chris." I never knew he was going to shoot, and I didn't think he would.' Against that denial (which of course, is the denial of a man in grievous peril) you will consider the evidence of the three police officers [Fairfax, McDonald and Harrison] who have sworn to you positively that those words were said.*

Counsel's argument was that Bentley's case, in Goddard's summing-up, amounted to one sentence, whereas the prosecution case, in Goddard's summing-up, 'covered some four or five pages'. This in Cassel's view, amounted to misdirection of the jury and ought to overturn the sentence. With a masterly disregard for fact, Croom-Johnson replied: 'Surely it is for the learned judge to decide what he is going to lay before the jury, and so long as it is done . . . fairly and squarely, that is sufficient.'**

But Croom-Johnson had clearly not been listening. Cassels's point was just that. The summing up had *not* been fair or square but Cassels was unable to shake their lordships on this.

The second appeal that Cassels put forward was more complicated, and it is still unresolved today. It was whether the joint adventure undertaken by Craig and Bentley had come to an end with the shooting of Miles. Again, common sense would indicate that the venture ceased to be joint the moment that Fairfax grabbed Bentley, at least for the second time. The panel of judges would not accept it. Neither would John Parris, Craig's Counsel, who wrote in *Most of My Murders* that the *consequences* of the joint venture could continue after the venture itself was over. For Parris then, the rejection of this second appeal was quite right, but the reasons for it were wrong.

Croom-Johnson said:

* *Notable British Trials* op. cit.
** Ibid

It is a little difficult for Mr Cassels because his own client was asked specifically at the hearing whether he was under arrest at the time when this shot, which killed Miles, was fired. He would not have it. He said he had not been under arrest, that the police officer had not detained him . . .*

This is patent nonsense. All that Bentley had said at the trial was that he was not under physical restraint (i.e. handcuffed or held down) all the time while on the roof; which is a far cry from Croom-Johnson's assertion.

For William Bentley, watching and listening to all this, it was incomprehensible. The legal moves swung this way and that, like a game of chess in which Derek was the pawn. The delay seemed – and seems – barbarous. The bewildered father did not feel competent to assess the judgement when it came. There were no grounds for Appeal. The original judgement stood. The family left the court in stunned silence, both Iris and her mother collapsing in the taxi on the way home. No sooner had they got there, than the phone rang. And kept on ringing. William Bentley did not answer it. He could talk to no one just then. He stuffed something between the clapper and the bell to silence the sound – the intrusion of the terrible, uncaring world outside.

From that day an extraordinary thing happened. The great British Public who had howled for the blood of a cosh boy; who were prepared to make a martyr out of Sidney Miles, now found a new cause: Derek Bentley. And the media, ever watchful, ever fickle, led them in a crusade such as the country had probably never seen before. The journalist Kenneth Allsop likened the days ahead to the mood of the country when the old king died, and saw a resolution in the cry 'Bentley must not die' which looked like the spirit of Dunkirk. The Bentley family had lashed each other closer and held on in the previous weeks. Now the cold stares and frosty silences became support, vocal and real. So many letters and telegrams arrived at Fairview Road, there had to be special deliveries and the only place to sort it all was in the bath. The phone never stopped. There was to be a public petition. Just in case the Home Secretary did not heed the jury's recommendation to mercy. In case Lord Goddard had not passed that recommendation on. In case. Just in case . . .

The actor Peter Ustinov and the film star Diana Dors were among

* *Notable British Trials* op. cit.

the famous names who rang or wrote to pledge support. Petition forms were printed and dispatched all over the country. They were returned within days, full and with requests for more. William Bentley, with Iris and Lilian, buried himself in a deluge of paperwork, meeting MPs and councillors, steeling himself against impressive people he might have found overbearing and, everywhere, meeting nothing but sympathy and kindness.

But in the end, sympathy and kindness could come from only one quarter – Sir David Maxwell-Fyfe, the Home Secretary. Without his acquiescence, all the petitions in the world, all the suggestions of 'reprieve Bentley' stickers and mass prayer meetings in Hyde Park would come to nothing. Lilian Bentley wrote to the Queen, the mother of a boy herself. She would understand.

They reached a crisis on 22 January, six days before the execution was due. Lilian had been facing up to the ordeal of the Wandsworth visits with enormous courage, but now there were signs that she could not take much more. That night she sat silently on Derek's bed in the room which had already become a shrine. Let William Bentley tell it:

> His clothes hung in the wardrobe. Under them were heaps of broken toys, books, comics and Bibles which he had collected over the years since early childhood. There was a Morse Code set, with a lamp attachment which we had given him as a birthday present.
>
> The impression of his head was still on the pillow which was slightly discoloured by the hair preparation he used.

A Biblical text hung over the bed – 'Casting all your care upon Him for He careth for you.' His hat and his jacket lay on the coverlet, his shoes tucked neatly under the bed on the linoleum that brightened the room. It looks quaint now, the photograph in William Bentley's book, like a moment frozen in history – the spartan utility furniture, the simple bed. No fitted carpet, no Walkman. No colour TV. Just a working-class bedroom at the end of rationing. Already a shrine.

It was while Lilian sat there that the real horror of the moment hit her husband. He did not interfere at times like these, but left her alone with her thoughts. Instead, he went to bed. The next day he would take the petition of 11,000 names to the Home Office. He couldn't sleep. He went downstairs and sent Iris up to her mother. As he sat, staring into the fire's dying embers, he suddenly knew that Derek was going to die:

I jumped from my chair [he wrote] to shake off the horror. Then I lost grip of my own identity. I did not know who I was. The familiar articles of furniture in the sitting room seemed strange. I went into the kitchen and filled a kettle to make tea. It was as if someone else was doing it and I was watching him from the outside . . . I came back, as it were, in flashes and with these lucid moments came the certainty that my son would be hanged. I can never hope to describe the horror; it was terrible beyond words.*

William and Iris were late getting to the Home Office because of the crowds of reporters clamouring for a statement. Two parcels of petitions out of the dozens they could have brought would be enough to make the point. And Bentley brought with him his own letter for the Home Secretary, containing eight points drafted by a legal adviser, which, in effect, spoke for the common sense and common justice which is the prerogative of every Englishman. Afterwards he made a statement to the Press, whose representatives were now arriving from the Commonwealth and America to cover the human interest of the story.

And the pressure now closed more directly on Maxwell-Fyfe. It came from a body of thirty Civil Servants who wrote to him on Bentley's behalf. It came from Dr Dennis Hill of the Maudsley Hospital who had examined Derek long before the trial, reminding the Home Secretary of the boy's epilepsy. And most extraordinary of all, it came from Sarah Bartley, an elderly lady living in Southend, who urged William Bentley by telegram to come to see her, as she was an invalid and could not travel.

The drowning William Bentley clutched at Sarah Bartley's straw. He hired a car and was driven east. 'I stared through the misted windows,' he wrote, 'seeing nothing but shadows of houses and blurs of coloured lights.' The lady who greeted him under the gaslights, with her long black dress, firm face and remarkable eyes, was the sister of Maxwell-Fyfe, the Home Secretary.

'I have written to him, asking him to spare your son's life. Have no fear, Mr Bentley, Derek will not die.'

But Derek did die. Was this purposeful, sincere old lady *really* the sister of the Home Secretary? To this day Iris Bentley believes she was. Or was she plain mad? Another of the ghouls who crawl out from the

* *My Son's Execution* by W. G. Bentley, 1957

woodwork at times like these, like the person who sent a hangman's noose to the Bentleys, wrapped in a shoe-box.

The next day, one of the reporters now permanently buzzing around 1 Fairview Road, asked the family for comment on the fact that Maxwell-Fyfe had not granted a reprieve. The news hit them like a bombshell. They had heard nothing. They frantically plunged their hands into the welter of unsorted mail in the bath and found it – the large buff envelope with the pompous initials OHMS. It was from Sir Frank Newsam, Maxwell-Fyfe's Under-Secretary, and it read:

> I am directed by the Secretary of State to inform you that he has given careful consideration to the petition submitted by you on behalf of your son, Derek Bentley, and I am to express to you his deep regret that after considering all the circumstances of the case he has failed to discover any sufficient ground to justify him in advising Her Majesty to interfere with the due course of law.*

Reluctantly, William Bentley read the letter to the others – 'I do not want to describe what happened to my wife and daughter after I had read the letter to them, but I shall hear their screams as long as I live.'

It was now Monday morning, 26 January. The letter had been posted on the Saturday and had not arrived until now. Such was the measure of Maxwell-Fyfe's 'deep regret'. In his autobiography *Political Adventure*, Maxwell-Fyfe, later Lord Kilmuir, said he believed that the fatal words Bentley spoke on the roof-top were 'Give it him, Chris.' He believed too that Craig had lodged an appeal. Such was the measure of Maxwell-Fyfe's 'careful consideration'.

The Bentleys went again to Wandsworth. Derek seemed to have lost the will to fight. He was pale, more strained than usual. His face crumpled as he sobbed into his chest beyond the glass partition 'Help me, please help me!' Men with more maturity than Derek Bentley have behaved this way, but his father would not let him down. He longed to smash through the glass to reach him. Iris and Lilian longed to hold him.

'When we leave here, Derek,' he told the boy, 'we shall do everything we can. People are working for you outside . . . You have thousands of friends, son. Trust us. We will do our best.'

Everything that the Bentleys could do came in two assaults. First, the

* Bentley op. cit.

surprising news that Mrs Craig had asked to see them. The parents had never met. They came from different social backgrounds. Only a Croydon roof-top had brought them together. William and Lilian walked to the Craig house in Norbury and somehow bore up as Mrs Craig told them of new evidence from Christopher, now in the Scrubs, that she had forwarded to Maxwell-Fyfe. A reporter took a photograph of the meeting. Mrs Craig, looking older than her years, taking the shattered Mrs Bentley by the hand. Posed and theatrical for the papers maybe, but the despair in Lilian Bentley's face says it all.

The Bentleys didn't sleep again that night. The next day, the eve of execution, they went with Mrs Craig to see Sir Frank Newsam, whose stenographer took down Christopher Craig's new evidence. It was not until later that day that the decision on this reached the Bentleys – in another pompous buff envelope Lilian Bentley had not dared to open.

> I am directed to inform you that the Secretary of State has given the fullest consideration to your representations but very much regrets that he has been unable to find any grounds for modifying the decision previously communicated to you.*

The substance of Christopher Craig's appeal on Bentley's behalf had been dismissed by the Home Secretary and has been dismissed by writers since as neither new nor evidence. It was perhaps neither of these things. But it was the truth.

William Bentley sent a telegram to Winston Churchill, the Prime Minister, taking a holiday on board the *Queen Mary* and about to return from the United States. He begged him to postpone the execution until his return. But Winnie was an old man, past his finest hour. He'd been a Home Secretary himself. He passed Bentley's telegram without comment back to Maxwell-Fyfe. This may have surprised William Bentley. It would not have surprised the people of Tonypandy in South Wales, who knew precisely Winston Churchill's attitude to justice.

All therefore rode on the second assault and this was delivered not by the Bentleys or the Craigs, but by a collection of MPs in the House itself. And their target was Maxwell-Fyfe. Francis Selwyn in *Gangland* reminds us how much the Home Secretary resembled Mussolini. A younger generation might see in him a clone of the comedian, Alexei

* Ibid

Sayle. In his wig as Lord Chancellor in the years after Craig and Bentley, he resembles a rather pompous poodle. One current judge has described him to me as a bully. Certainly, he was an unprepossessing Home Secretary in an unprepossessing Cabinet, headed by a man now more old than grand and dominated, if that is the right word, by a Foreign Secretary who brought us the humiliation of Suez. And Ludovic Kennedy recounts, in his recent autobiography, the jingle of the Bar of those days:

> The nearest thing to death in life
> Is David Patrick Maxwell-Fyfe.

Bogged down as he was in the opening weeks of the year with a Welsh debate on the effects of the new steel works at Margam, Maxwell-Fyfe suddenly found himself confronted with a decision over Derek Bentley. On the afternoon of Tuesday 27 January, Sidney Silverman, the short, stocky, white-haired MP for Nelson and Colne rose in the Commons to ask the Speaker, W. S. Morrison, why the motion he had tabled on the Bentley execution was not printed on the Order Paper. The House was packed. Silverman's mailbag was running at 200 to 1 in favour of reprieve, like some insane horse-race where Derek Bentley might lose by a neck. Telegrams arrived for Silverman as he spoke and tumbled like large confetti over bench and floor. Morrison explained that the motion had been denied because it would be unconstitutional in effect for MPs to harass the Home Secretary while he was deliberating the issue. Silverman pointed out that Maxwell-Fyfe had already made his decision and that this was a direct challenge of that decision.

Amid a tumult of noise the House settled into the pace so familiar to all of us who have watched such squabbles. It became a party matter. Derek Bentley in these minutes was not a human being. He was political capital. Reginald Paget, Labour MP for Northampton was on his feet, ripping into Maxwell-Fyfe and the abhorrent system he represented –

> I think the great condemnation which we made of the German people was that they stood aside and did nothing when dreadful things happened. We are a sovereign assembly. A three-quarter-witted boy of nineteen is to be hanged for a murder he did not commit and which was committed fifteen minutes after he was

arrested. Can we be made to keep silence when a thing as horrible and as shocking as this is to happen?*

The baying and the insults worsened. MPs were on their feet, waving papers, hurling abuse at Maxwell-Fyfe and at the Speaker, who was accused of collusion, of protecting a Minister of the Crown. Morrison would not be swayed. He ruled that according to the customs of the House the matter of the correctness of Bentley's execution could only be discussed after it had been carried out. The nightmare had reached Brobdingnagian proportions. Silverman scribbled out a motion for adjournment, demanding that attention be drawn to a 'definite matter of urgent public importance'. Morrison refused to accept it. Even with the redoubtable Aneurin Bevan at Silverman's side, he would not be shaken. The anger subsided. Whatever passion men like Silverman and Paget and Bevan brought to the day, however strongly they felt, Derek Bentley was less important to the House in general than other issues. With a callousness difficult to accept even in the Conservative post-war era, they drifted on to an Argentinian trade debate. Silverman had left the Chamber to report the melancholy news to William Bentley.

But the phalanx for reprieve would not give up. A six-man deputation spearheaded by Silverman, Bevan and Lyn Ungoed-Thomas, a former Solicitor-General, took a petition personally to Maxwell-Fyfe. The Home Secretary was impressed, as no one could fail to be, by Bevan's arguments, but perhaps he remembered that Nye Bevan had once referred to the Metropolitan Police College at Hendon as a 'Fascist institution'. And one of the duties of this man was to command the police. Maxwell-Fyfe considered the new petition and deputation, both delivered in all good faith, gave Bevan a considered reply by quarter to ten at night and went home.

He had said nothing during the stormy debates in the Chamber. He had sat with his arms folded across his black coat, Anthony Eden at his elbow. There had been no glimmer of expression on his face. Why did he not give way to the obvious pressure on him, both in the House and in the country at large? He had been receiving threatening letters and phone calls. One lady, who may in fact have been Sarah Bartley, rang every half hour from Monday the 26th until the Post Office cut off all calls. The police presence around Maxwell-Fyfe and his wife Sylvia was increased. And the Maxwell-Fyfes were able to smile at the

---

* *Hanged and Innocent?* by R. T. Paget & S. S. Silverman, London 1953

'sporadic injustice' of the fact that when a large, hostile crowd threatened to attack what they thought was the Home Secretary's house, only the ageing Labour peer Lord Silkin was there and found himself trying to calm an angry mob.

'His reasoning,' Maxwell-Fyfe's widow, the Dowager Countess de la Warr, was to recall to Fenton Bresler years later, 'as I remember it was that if a young man of Bentley's age got off because he went on that kind of enterprise with an even younger man who did not hang, it would happen again. It would be an encouragement to similar exploits in the future.'*

And David Maxwell-Fyfe was not the type to give in to bullying, least of all bullying by public opinion. If a Home Secretary gave way to that, then his entire office held no meaning at all. So in the end the 'man who rations mercy' offered no mercy at all. He ignored the jury's recommendation. He ignored Goddard who had assured his maid at the height of this pro-Bentley hysteria that she needn't worry – Bentley would not hang.

Before either of these assaults on the bastion of the Establishment had finished, the Bentleys had gone to see their son for the last time. Derek was cheerful, teasing Iris about the eyeshadow she was wearing. He was calm, asking after the rheumatism of a neighbour. Lilian gave him a newspaper cutting of his pet dogs, a letter from a friend and a rosary. William Bentley felt waves of weakness passing over him. Like the breakers on the beach, they swept on and over his exhausted brain. Derek told him off, laughingly, for grinding his teeth.

'The last moment with him was the worst,' William Bentley was to write, 'I can see him now as he called out – "Cheerio, Dad! Cheerio, Mum! Cheerio, Iris!"'

'And we walked away.

' "See you tomorrow . . ."'

'Those were the last words we heard him speak.'

And that night, as the Commons went home and Maxwell-Fyfe had his phone unplugged again, the crowds gathered, angry, dark, vengeful. Where was the compassion in all of this? The humanity? None of it made any sense. There was a crowd of hundreds jammed into Fairview Road, besieging the little end of terrace house. They cheered and applauded the Bentleys home. Others began moving along the Embankment. Still more towards Downing Street. Number 10, the

* *Lord Goddard* by Fenton Bresler, London 1977

Home Office, even Buckingham Palace, were all potential targets. A phone call to the Bentleys' house talked of a march to see the Queen. Banners, placards were ready. Would the Bentleys lead them? A wheelchair was arranged for Mrs Bentley if she couldn't walk.

It was the stuff of Peterloo and St Petersburg's Bloody Sunday — naïve and bewildered people, from all ranks of society, pensioners rubbing shoulders with kids, stumbling around in the darkness in a vain, a hopeless quest for mercy. And for something else. For justice. This was a long time before the age of protest in the 60's, when people took to the streets, as they still do to campaign for the 'unborn gay whale'. Such a movement was spontaneous, from the heart. And it was dangerous. A second call to the Bentleys' was, ironically, from the authorities. The crowds were in an ugly mood and growing by the hour. And so it was that William Bentley and the twenty-one-year-old Iris, who had spent the three hundred pounds put aside for her forthcoming wedding on Derek's cause, tramped the dark, cold night, from crowd to crowd, calling for calm, calling for order:

'My family and I thank you from the bottom of our hearts. We shall always be grateful to you. But nothing more can be done. My son is now in God's hands.'

Be discreet and respectable at all times; avoid attracting public attention going to or from the prison; report at prison before four o'clock in the afternoon; be available for interview by Governor; receive physical details of prisoner from Governor; inspect; select and test apparatus by engineer; view prisoner without prisoner being aware; stretch rope; inform Governor of length of drop; final adjustment of rope next morning . . .*

This was the routine specified by the Home Office for the execution of the condemned. It was more or less invented by a quiet, professional little man called Albert Pierrepoint, the last public executioner in Britain. He had come a long way from the barbarous mistakes of William Calcraft and the not-much-better James Berry, two of Victoria's executioners. His was a precise science. He had got to get it right.

While Silverman was on his feet in the Commons, Pierrepoint

* *Executioner: Pierrepoint* by Albert Pierrepoint, London 1974

[95]

watched his man through the Judas Hole, the tiny peep-hole from the connecting execution shed into Bentley's cell. He did not, as some writers have suggested, make notes on him. He did not meet him or shake his hand to gauge his weight and strength. Derek Bentley was tall – 6 feet, 4 inches – but his wiry strength was superficial. The photographs taken by Iris of Derek posing in the garden with lard smeared over his biceps have added to the myth of a powerful man.

Pierrepoint was ready. There was a large crowd at the main gates of Wandsworth, swaying, chanting their anger. 'Be discreet and respectable at all times; avoid attracting public attention . . .'

'It was a damp, raw morning,' William Bentley remembered, 'the sky was livid.'

Under that same sky, a couple of miles away at Wandsworth, a thousand people pressed the great studded gates. Were there enough of them to break in? Would mob violence succeed where reason and oratory had failed? And while hell broke loose outside, inside, Pierrepoint went about his business.

At five to nine a knot of people gathered outside the condemned cell. C. R. Wigan, the Under-Sheriff of Surrey, headed the group. He had been in place for fifteen minutes in accordance with the Home Office directive. With him were James Murdoch, Wandsworth's Medical Officer; the Governor, W. J. Lawton; the Chaplain, the Reverend Ball; two warders, ready to drag or carry the boy if they had to; a hospital orderly in case he fainted; and a prison engineer, who, with Pierrepoint and his assistant, managed the nuts and bolts of the mechanism.

At twenty seconds to nine by his pocket watch, Wigan gave the signal, breaking the silence which Pierrepoint never wanted to break, 'the communication only by a lift of the finger or a slight nod of the head.'*

Outside, the vast, swaying crowd fell silent. Mrs Van der Elst, an ardent campaigner against capital punishment, had arrived in her yellow Rolls-Royce. She had been denied access to Governor Lawton, for all her wealth and connections. The shouts of 'Murder!' died away and an eerie stillness fell.

'Let us be with him in his moment of need,' she said softly. Slowly, as if in a dream, trilbies and bowlers and cloth caps were tugged from heads. Those heads bowed and on the chill air of the morning the

---

* Pierrepoint op. cit.

'The threequarter-witted boy' who went to Croydon
'just for the ride'

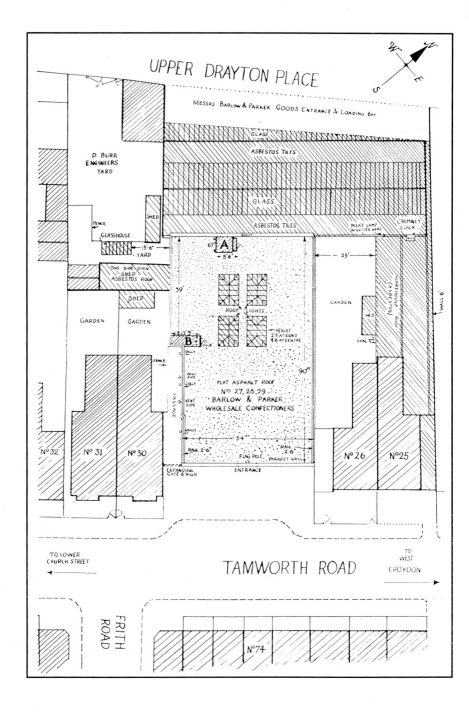

The police plan of the Barlow and Parker warehouse
produced at the Old Bailey

Constable Claude Pain of Z Division, Metropolitan Police
with his dog 'Wolf', East Croydon Station, 1954

Claude Pain (centre) helps the injured Christopher Craig
into Croydon Magistrates' Court

Constable Sidney Miles, the man with 'a ton of guts' who
died on a Croydon rooftop, Sunday 2 November 1952

Rayner Goddard, the Lord Chief Justice of England, attending
a ceremony for the opening of the Michaelmas Law Sittings
three years before the Craig and Bentley case

Derek Bentley in custody, 'so proud of his waves'
but bewildered by flashing cameras

The verdict is out. Harry Proctor of the *Sunday Pictorial*
whisks Mrs Craig and her daughter Lucy away from
the Old Bailey, 11 December 1952

The 'conspicuously brave' policemen who faced Craig's bullets on the Croydon rooftop.
L. to R : Constable Norman Harrison, Detective-Sergant Frederick Fairfax,
Constable James McDonald, Constable Robert Jaggs

'Let's get the murderers!' The crowd tries to force the main gate of Wandsworth Prison on the announcement of Bentley's execution, 28 January 1953

'Lest we forget': William, Lilian and Iris Bentley placing a wreath
outside Wandsworth Prison on the twentieth anniversary of Derek's death

The plumber who has gone ex-directory,
Christopher Craig photographed in the summer of 1989

ragged tune struggled upwards, lonely, unaccompanied: 'Abide with me; fast falls the eventide . . .'

At 1, Fairview Road, what was left of the Bentleys clung together – William, Lilian, Iris and little Denis. 'Oranges and Lemons' broke over the Light Programme airwaves. They held each other close, standing as though in that execution shed. 'The stroke of the first hour crashed and filled the room,' echoing in their hearts and in their heads until they thought that both would break.

At Wandsworth, Pierrepoint and his assistant entered the cell. They moved mechanically, accustomed to the drill. They pinioned Derek's arms behind his back with the special strap Pierrepoint's father had devised. No one spoke. No one shook hands. Close-lipped though he has remained about these things, Pierrepoint was to write later that Bentley did not cry. His dad, his mum, Iris, all of them, would be proud of him. They put his feet on the marked spots so that each stood on a different flap of the doors. The drill rattled again through Pierrepoint's brain: 'Draw on the white cap, adjust the noose, whip out the safety pin, push the lever, drop . . .'* It had been instilled into him when he was about to become an executioner at the age of twenty-seven, when he worked clumsily on a dummy, ironically called 'Old Bill'.

'On the actual job you're dealing with human flesh. You've got to get it right . . .'**

Pierrepoint's assistant dropped to the floor. He pinioned Derek's legs and jumped aside. For a split second, Pierrepoint checked to see the platform was clear. He could see Ball praying to his left, the white hood over Bentley's head billowing and closing as he fought for breath for one last time.

'Cap, noose, pin, push, drop . . .'***

The last chime of the hour sounded. It had taken between nine and twelve seconds from the time Pierrepoint had entered the cell. The white rope hung taut, creaking on its housings.

He had got it right.

The prison breathed again. A warder appeared at the gate and put up a notice. No public circus. That was stopped in 1868. No black flag. Not

* Pierrepoint op. cit.
** Ibid
*** Ibid

since 1907. Only a flimsy piece of official prison stationery, swiftly typed.

> We, the undersigned, hereby declare that judgement of death was this day executed on Derek William Bentley in Her Majesty's Prison of Wandsworth, in our presence.*

This fanned the crowd to anger again. The haunting refrain of 'The Lord's my Shepherd' gave way to shouts and jostling. 'Let's get the murderers!' The glass case housing the execution notice was smashed and all but ripped from the gates. Coins and apple cores were thrown at the cordon of police who fought with the demonstrators, backs to the wall. But the gates were closed again and the damage had been done. People put on their hats and began to drift away.

'To such public indignation,' wrote William Bentley, 'the baby I had helped to deliver just over nineteen years before went out of this world'.

The body of Derek Bentley hung in the execution shed for the traditional one hour, to ensure that life was extinct. At the end of that time, Murdoch, the Medical Officer, went with Pierrepoint to lift him down. This was not the Croydon roof-top. It was not the dock of the Bailey. This time he needed help.

The pathologist David Haler carried out a post-mortem in the prison morgue. He found Bentley's brain to be 'perfectly normal' and that death had occurred as a result of 'judicial hanging'. This was the official finding of the requisite jury – a formality. If Pierrepoint's measurements had been correct, Bentley's neck would have snapped at the third vertebra and death would have been instantaneous.

'The law is a machine,' wrote William Bentley, 'that grinds out life and death and good and ill. It has no heart.'

He went to Wandsworth to claim Derek's clothes, the new ones he had bought him for the trial. He was told they had been burnt. It was the custom. Just as it was the custom that the dead boy had been buried in a cheap coffin somewhere in the grounds of the prison, at lunch-time when the prisoners were in the refectory and the hasty shovelling of earth would not be noticed. Even by the end of July of that year, the

* Bentley op. cit.

practice of clothes-burning had been discontinued and such clothes were in future to be returned to next of kin. 'The law is a machine . . . It has no heart.'

It was now that Silverman caught the Speaker out in a lie. Morrison had voiced no objection to the Bentley case being discussed after the execution. Yet when Silverman tried again, he was again denied justice. All that was left for him now was to go into print and later that year, with Reginald Paget, he wrote *Hanged – and Innocent?* It was the first of many books written in an attempt to throw light on the case. Paget, responsible for the chapter on Bentley, cites five reasons for the Home Secretary to have granted a reprieve. First, the consideration of youth. The law said that no one under the age of eighteen could be hanged. It was traditional for those near eighteen to be spared. At nineteen and a half was Derek Bentley simply too old for this tradition? Second, that where the 'leading actor' (i.e. Craig) in a case of murder could not be hanged, neither should his accomplice. Third, Bentley's low intelligence and epilepsy put him measurably near the McNaghten Rules covering the fitness of a criminal to plead. Fourth, two Parliamentary commissions, in 1839 and 1878, had recommended that such cases as Bentley's where death was caused without malice ought to be reviewed – the law in fact should be rewritten. Finally, wherever there was a 'scintilla' of doubt, the practice was to reprieve. The fact that Maxwell-Fyfe ignored all five points led Paget to conclude that the only consideration the Home Secretary had had in mind was that of a new, unwritten and undisclosed doctrine. A policeman had been killed. *Somebody* had to hang. And Maxwell-Fyfe was the man who commanded the police. We may not accept Paget's description of 'a drooling, dim-witted Bentley' but there are few who would deny that 'his execution was a supreme indecency'.

There is controlled anger in this book, as there is in the second one to appear: *My Son's Execution*, by William Bentley. But there is tenderness here, too. And an overwhelming sense of bewilderment and loss. Bentley had difficulty in interesting publishers. After all the shouting had died down, Bentley was the father of a convicted felon, in the eyes of the law every bit as guilty of murder as Christopher Craig. It was an unattractive picture and those publishers who shook their heads were no doubt of the same school as Maxwell-Fyfe, who now congratulated himself on the fact that his mailbag in the days after the execution praised him for his courage and the rightness of his decision. In the end, he was even able to describe himself as the underdog! W. H. Allen became interested, however, and approached Bentley. The result is one of the most moving books ever written, moving in the sense that it is the honest reflection of a working man caught up in a nightmare. And if there are times when he paints his goose as a swan, what father does not? Certainly *My Son's Execution* ought to be compulsory reading for anyone with a child growing up in a dangerous and hostile world. And for anyone who wants to see a return of the rope.

Three years later, John Parris, Craig's counsel, went into print with *Most of my Murders*. The enigmatic Mr Parris and his 'third boy' theory will be discussed in a later chapter. He had been working with Iris Bentley on a full-scale book of the case which was to have been published the year after *My Son's Execution*, but it was not to be and became absorbed as one of twelve chapters illustrating Parris's career. By this time, Parris had been disbarred for being an active member of a trading company, and he was freer to discuss the many anomalies of the case than he had been when a careless, rather defamatory reference to Lord Goddard immediately after the trial led to some months suspension from the Bar. In the same year the lawyer C. G. L. Du Cann wrote *Miscarriages of Justice*, which examined the Bentley case in eleven pages, nearly half of which were given over to discussion of a point of law only obliquely relevant.

It was not until 1971 that the first full-length work appeared, David Yallop's *To Encourage the Others*. All subsequent writers owe a debt of gratitude to Mr Yallop, who has a deserved reputation for tackling a wide range of true crime with gusto and a meticulous eye for detail. In the end, however, his 'startling new facts' are not actual facts at all, but hypothesis. And however fascinating, cannot be supported. The book caused a sensation when it first appeared and led to extensive media coverage, not to mention the threats at least of libel suits. To this day, Yallop regards the Bentley case as 'his' and treats outsiders with scant regard.

Stumbling into the arena in 1988 came the journalist Francis Selwyn with the inappropriately titled *Gangland*. It is difficult to see why this book was published at all. It is really just a synthesis of all that had gone before – a very tired technique – and as such tends to perpetuate errors (I counted twelve important ones). Selwyn has Christopher Craig in non-contemporary drainpipe trousers and the childless Sidney Miles the father of two children. He delights in writing newspaper banner headlines in block capitals, but the main thrust of the book seems to be that, contrary to earlier theses, comics and cinema had little causal effect on the behaviour of Craig and Bentley, which merely takes us back to 1952 and Lord Goddard's contention at the trial.

Dad Help Me Please, published in January 1990 by the same publisher who took on William Bentley, treads more old, familiar ground. It too is riddled with errors and the authors Christopher Berry-Dee and the distinguished crime writer Robin Odell, claim to have found hitherto undisclosed Home Office papers which were released to Berry-Dee by mistake. Clearly, Mr Berry-Dee was luckier in his researches than I. These papers were in fact released to Iris Bentley years ago and were therefore available for public scrutiny at any time. Unfortunately, the wait was not really worth it. *Dad Help Me Please* takes 164 pages to make a point that David Yallop made nineteen years ago in a few lines –

'. . . these were the issues [the ability of Bentley to plead] that should have been clarified in front of the Old Bailey jury and *never* were. The issue was never raised.' (Mr Yallop's italics).

The Appendix of the Berry-Dee book, dealing with the ballistics evidence, is highly technical, but it is based essentially on the *assumption* of when Craig actually reloaded his gun and in the absence of the fatal bullet which killed Miles, can still only be conjecture.

The book is undoubtedly very sympathetic towards Derek Bentley, but there would seem to be about as much chance for a posthumous pardon out of it as spitting in the wind.

It is in the world beyond books that the cause of Derek Bentley has been kept curiously alive. Mention the case to most people old enough to know it and it is the name of Ludovic Kennedy they remember. In his recently published autobiography, *On My Way To The Club*, Kennedy relates how he and his wife, like many other people, were shocked and appalled by Maxwell-Fyfe's decision. He wrote a play (*Murder Story*) which revolves around a character based on Derek Bentley who learns to read and write in the condemned cell. It was produced on the London stage by Peter Haddon and played to rave reviews and weeping audiences. William Bentley and his daughter were less impressed. They went to the first night and didn't like it. For them, it wasn't, it couldn't be, Derek. Although the play subsequently appeared in book form, the stage run was short. Astutely, Kennedy observes that London audiences don't like their consciences being pricked.

David Yallop's book was taken up by an enthusiastic BBC in a drama-documentary in 1972. A number of policemen in Croydon at the time of the roof-top incident bombarded the switchboard with complaints of inaccuracy.

What of the Bentley family and their forlorn search for justice? Shortly before Christmas 1953 – the second Christmas the Bentleys spent without their eldest son – William Bentley met Sir Frank Newsam again at the Home Office, and asked permission to be allowed to place flowers on Derek's grave. The Home Secretary was still the immovable David Maxwell-Fyfe. The answer was no. And so, on 28 January each year, a little cohort made up of a working class family went to the grey, grim gates of Wandsworth and placed flowers and a card, written until her death in 1978 by Lilian Bentley – 'In Loving Memory of my Son'.

The torch now has passed to Iris Bentley. I was first to have met this brave, extraordinary lady on 28 January 1989. It was not to be because Iris Bentley is far from well. Her father, who died in 1974, described her as a semi-invalid twenty years earlier. She suffered from nightmares in which she saw Derek at the foot of her bed. But Iris Bentley is stronger even than her father knew. She promised her parents that she would carry on the fight to prove Derek's innocence for the rest of her life if need be. Her daughter Maria has taken up the torch too, for the memory of the 'Uncle Derek' she never knew. The Friends of Derek Bentley, organized principally by Yallop in the early Seventies, were instrumental with Iris and Maria in visiting local schools and youth clubs with the cautionary tale of a 'three-quarter-witted boy' inveigled all too easily into crime. At nine and a half years of age, Maria was talking to children all over South London about the case. Until 1973 when the place was closed down by a Conservative council, the Cockpit Theatre, Marylebone was the venue for discussions which played their part in reducing juvenile delinquency. In that year, two of our more 'compassionate' politicians, Norman Tebbit and Michael Brotherton complained about what they saw as a misuse of time and funds. *The Times* quoted Tebbit –

'I can think of nothing more undesirable than sending people with an axe to grind to lecture to impressionable people on that particular subject.'

And Brotherton –

'It is disgusting that public money should be used to provide a platform for one who seeks to justify a convicted murderer of a policeman.'

The Inner London Education Authority pointed out that Iris Bentley did not presume to lecture on law and order and that she received no payment at all. She was merely part of a team composed of actors and teachers and answered questions from children who had already made a study of the issues involved. I wonder how much difference that made to Messrs Tebbit and Brotherton who did, after all, represent the political party of David Maxwell-Fyfe. From 1977 to '79 the gentle musical *Lullaby For Mrs Bentley*, written by Stephen Wyatt, played in the King's Head Theatre Club, Islington, then Manchester. And from 1979 to 1980 Richard Ireson's *Bentley* ran at the Warehouse Theatre, London.

When I began to write this book people told me not to trust Iris Bentley. 'She's out for what she can get,' they said. Perhaps they're right. Because what Iris Bentley wants is justice. They moved the mortal remains of Derek Bentley from the anonymous mould of Wandsworth to Croydon Cemetery on 4 March 1968, only a few yards from where they scattered the ashes of Sidney Miles. What Iris Bentley wants is to have chiselled on her brother's headstone – 'Derek Bentley. A victim of British justice.' The authorities will not allow it. What Iris Bentley wants is for a ward to be named after her brother at the Great Ormond Street Hospital for Sick Children. Derek Bentley was a child himself.

At the beginning and at the end of this book are two songs written about Craig and Bentley. The first is by the folk singer Ralph McTell for a performance at Croydon to commemorate the thirtieth anniversary of the case. It does not pretend to be an accurate account –

Back at Fell Road they signed the rifles out . . .*

But it catches the hopes of Iris Bentley –

Oh you men on our behalf who sanctioned that boy's death,
There's still one thing left to do.

* © Misty River Music 1982

You can pardon Derek Bentley who never took a life
For Derek Bentley cannot pardon you.*

The second was written by the pop star Elvis Costello and performed on his album 'Spike' as I was writing this book. Its notes are not as haunting as McTell's but its image is as powerful –

They say Derek Bentley was easily led,
Well, what's that to the woman that Sidney Miles wed?**

And Costello echoes the views of Albert Pierrepoint, who doubted in the end that hanging served any point other than the ritual, vicious lust by society for revenge:

From a Welfare State to society murder
'Bring back the noose' is always heard
Whenever those swine are under attack,
But it won't make you even,
It won't bring him back,
Let him dangle.***

Derek Bentley has passed into folklore. But why did he 'pass' at all? How was it that a gentle boy, virtually vegetarian because he was so fond of animals; a boy who was 'easily led'; a boy who was under arrest when somebody else committed the crime in question, could be put to death?

Let us go back to the December of 1952.

* © Misty River Music 1982
** © Plangent Visions Music Inc. ASCAP
*** Ibid

—— 5 ——

THE TRIAL OF THE CENTURY

At the beginning of the Craig and Bentley trial Mr Christmas Humphreys, Counsel for the Prosecution, reminded the jury that they were to decide the case on the issues as they were put before them in the court, not as they had appeared before them in the newspapers. The problem for any researcher is the bewildering overlay of nonsense created by the Press. Quite apart, that is, from the legalized fiction of the court-room.

It is a chilling experience to read the newspapers relating to the case and an interesting realization that the national press is appreciably wider of the mark than the local press. In the era of the cosh boy, sensationalism was easy. And the great British public never tired of buying it. For sheer unadulterated nonsense, the prize belongs to the *Daily Mail*, its lurid headline 'Chicago gun battle in London: gangsters with machine-guns on a roof kill detective, wound another: "Sidney Street" rages an hour, then hand-to-hand fight. Armed police shoot back' –

> The London crime wave reached a new peak last night. A detective [*sic*] was shot dead and another seriously [*sic*] wounded in a second 'Battle of Sidney Street' [*sic*]. They had seen the flash of a torchlight in [*sic*] the warehouse of Barlow and Parker, wholesale confec-tioners, Tamworth Road, Croydon, just after ten o'clock [*sic*]. They entered the building [*sic*]. They cautiously edged their way in [*sic*]. Inside [*sic*] the raiders were so far undisturbed [*sic*]. Ambulances and fire brigades had been summoned. Then as the bandits realized they had been trapped by a police cordon, shooting began. The gangsters armed with a Sten-gun [*sic*!] hit one of the officers as he climbed the fire escape [*sic*] towards the bandits. He was Detective [*sic*] Constable Miles, in plain clothes [*sic*] of Z Division, a married

man, two children [sic] with 22 years service. He was killed. His colleague PC [sic] Frederick Fairfax, who was in a police patrol car [sic] dashed into an alleyway leading to another fire escape [sic] up which the gunman had climbed. As he went to help Miles there was another shot and people coming out of the Sunday cinemas heard one of the gunmen cry 'You won't get me'. PC Fairfax fell wounded in the shoulder. By this time 200 police were there, thirty [sic] of them armed with revolvers. Shots were exchanged. . . . Then the end came. As three [sic] officers crouching low, sprung on to the rooftop, the Sten-gun was flung in their faces [sic]. The ammunition had run out. Then began a chase over the roofs [sic] after the gunmen. They dodged behind chimney pots [sic]. One of them attempted to lower himself by a stackpipe [sic] at the rear of the premises. By this time more police were on the roofs, and there were hand-to-hand battles [sic] before the two gunmen [sic] were finally overpowered, handcuffed and brought to street level . . .

Yallop makes the point fairly enough that the two reporters responsible should have received 'some kind of inverted Pulitzer Prize for a historic piece of misreporting'. Add up the [sic]s above and you will see that there are twenty-five of them. It reads in fact like the synopsis of a gangster B feature that Craig might have gone to see. What is tragic is that this purported to be the truth. It was this garbled nonsense which judge and counsel at the trial urged the jury to disregard and which of course it was impossible for them to disregard. Human psychology does not work like that and it is one of the great weaknesses of our legal system. Every one of the jury who sat in No. 2 court of the Old Bailey that December had preconceived ideas on Craig and Bentley, ideas which they had gleaned from newspaper articles like the one above. No wonder the crowd jostled the injured Craig at Croydon Magistrates' Court; no wonder the papers, national and local, rang with the baying of the mob.

The *Daily Express*, traditionally the rival of the *Mail* in the Fleet Street jungle, was rather more accurate in its reporting. It carried a clear head and shoulders photograph of Sidney Miles. On Monday, 3 November, Lord Beaverbrook's chained crusader cost 1½d. and the weather forecast was of bright spells with showers. There was a front page spread devoted to the incident of the previous night and nine-year-old Pearl Ware was posed at her bedroom window with her mother. Around the lurid headlines there was talk of a 'little airlift' in

Berlin, now that Churchill's 'iron curtain' had descended. Dwight Eisenhower was days away from election as America's thirty-fourth President, and proposed to fly on a peace mission to war-torn Korea. The impending speech of the new Queen to Parliament was found to cause alarm – transport and iron and steel were to be denationalized; there was to be drastic modification of land development changes; the rearmament programme was to be reorganized on its first faltering steps towards Armageddon; and most shocking of all, one supposes, to some of the London commuters who read all this while strap-hanging, there were to be further cuts in the Civil Service.

It was all dwarfed, however, by the lead story. But even here, inaccuracies abound. Craig and Bentley were described as a gun gang, giving the totally false impression built upon by Francis Selwyn in his *Gangland*. Bentley's age is given as 22 and both Miles and Fairfax reached the roof by means of a fireman's ladder. Fairfax is again described as Police rather than Detective Constable, and they both arrived at Tamworth Road in the same vehicle, the first on the scene. Even Miles's address – Sundial Road – is incorrect.

As interesting as contemporary national press write-ups of the roof-top gun battle, are the letters and comments from the public. With marvellous understatement, in what was obviously a running series called 'Here's a job I wouldn't like', Anthony G. Tanery of Ruthin, North Wales, wrote: 'My vote goes to the policeman, with all these cosh boys and thugs about.'

The letters page is dominated by the violent playground issue. Of every hundred letters received by the *Express*, only two did not urge the return of flogging for crimes of violence. Echoing the views of the 'impartial' Lord Chief Justice, Cyril Tanner of Birmingham wrote: 'Assaults reported in the Daily Express made shocking reading. The moment is *now* for the return of birching. Give the courts the power at once.' Donald McLeod of Glasgow went further: '. . . cosh boys? Don't birch 'em – shoot 'em.' And the 'caring' words of Canon Dudley Symon of St Michael's Convent, Ham Common, Middlesex, have a rather incongruous ring, bearing in mind the man's pastoral calling:

> . . . even imprisonment, which used to be more varied, has been brought in these Socialistic days to a dead level. There is now no 'hard labour' but the same form for all customers and 'all wery comfortable' (as Sam Weller would have said) except for over-crowding.

Our ancestors however had a much greater variety at their disposal. They went in for branding, nose slitting, ear cropping, whipping at the cart's tail, ducking in the village pond (for women), the pillory, the stocks; while in the eighteenth century there was also deportation. *Some* [my italics] of these no doubt are best forgotten. But we might learn from them to go in for a little more variety than at present we seem capable of and also to inquire whether a revival of the pillory and the stocks might not be a very useful thing ... The stocks might now be used for litter fiends among others ... The pillory would be appropriate for black marketeers, petty swindlers, inconsiderate drivers, people cruel to animals and the like.

Imprisonment should clearly be divided into different types and the element of 'hard labour' (possibly in labour camps) reintroduced.

It is a pity that deportation is no longer possible. An island in the Pacific seems good enough for some of the types Lord Goddard described provided the islanders did not object.

Lastly, would it be possible to divide capital punishment into two forms: 'honourable' and 'dishonourable'? No-one wants to hang a hopeless criminal lunatic: but would not a pleasant euthanasia be just, both to him and to society?

Punishment must not only deter and reform; it must vindicate justice and uphold society.

By January 1953 they had hanged Derek Bentley, who no doubt in some people's eyes would fit the good Canon's description of 'a hopeless criminal lunatic'. By 1963 the Canon would probably have been mortified to learn that they had released Christopher Craig without his having undergone any hard labour at all. But the reader who is surprised, perhaps even mildly outraged, by the Canon's views should be sobered by the fact that there was a long history of such sentiment in the Church. Canon Charles Kingsley of *The Water Babies* fame believed the natives of Sarawak sub-human because they were not Christian, and regularly belted his wife with a cat o' nine tails. Further back still, it is the stuff on both sides of the Reformation, the universal language of the Inquisition.

And fascinatingly, bearing in mind the comic-strip influence on boys like Craig, and the image of the policeman referred to in Chapter 3, tucked away on the back page of the *Express* are the adventures of

Sergeant Flint of the Flying Squad. Not surprisingly, our man Flint has a trilby hat, a trenchcoat and a lantern jaw.

The local papers like the *Croydon Times* and the *Croydon Advertiser* carry a great deal more detail and veracity. Admittedly the smoke of battle had cleared by Friday, 7 November, when the *Advertiser* appeared, and local men could perhaps be expected to get the facts straighter. It is an axiom, however, that reportage in most local newspapers is often only average and this must offset the extravagances of Fleet Street.

Details of the hearing at Number One Magistrates' Court, Croydon, on Monday, 3 November, are illuminating on contemporary attitudes. Bentley was described as a well-built youth, which is not really apparent from his photographs, and he appeared in the dock with a 'highly coloured shirt, with no tie, and a sports jacket'. These of course were the clothes he was wearing when he went out 'for a walk' with Norman Parsley. One can almost hear the sneer in the description. Interestingly, he is described as an electrician, almost certainly because of his father's radio repair shop. The court was crowded as Bentley was brought up the steps via an underground passage from the old police station across the road from the Town Hall. The only witness to give evidence at this hearing was Detective Chief Inspector John Smith. Outside in the corridor, waiting to give the evidence that no one has heard until now, sat Police Constable Claude Pain. He was never called. Smith told the court:

At 5.30 a.m. today I saw accused detained at Croydon Police Station. I said to him 'I am a police officer and I have just seen the body of PC Sidney George Miles at Mayday Mortuary lying dead. As a result of inquiries I have made, I am going to charge you with being concerned with Christopher Craig in murdering him at Tamworth Road about 9.30 p.m. yesterday.'

I cautioned him and he said 'Craig shot him. I have not got a gun. He was with me on the roof and shot him then, between the eyes.'

He was charged and again cautioned and he made no reply. On that evidence I ask for a remand in custody until next Monday.*

The Clerk of the Court, Mr O. Milan, had already read the charge to Bentley and Bentley had answered, 'Not me, sir.' The Chairman of the

* *Croydon Advertiser*

Court, Mr B. W. N. Still, asked Bentley if he had any questions for the inspector. He did not. He asked him if there was any reason why Bentley should not be remanded in custody. There was not.

'Do you still want legal aid?' Still asked.

'I will see my father,' Bentley replied.*

William, Lilian and Iris Bentley sat as near to him as they could in the crowded room. As the only means of communication available to them in this frightening, incomprehensible nightmare, Iris used the lip-reading game that she and Derek had played as children. Moving his lips slightly before he entered the dock, he told her he was desperate for a cigarette. And then Iris watched the lips of various policemen in the court . . .

It was the start of W. G. Bentley's long, desperate, and in the end hopeless struggle to save his son. Bentley junior was led away through the underground passage to the station and about two hours later, driven to Brixton prison to await trial. The hearing had lasted six minutes.

And the inaccuracies in the Press continued. Ex-Captain of the Army Transport Corps, Frederick Fairfax, is described as a Commando Captain, no doubt to underscore his roof-top heroics and the ease with which he subdued Bentley. A firearm was *reached up to him* [my italics] as he reached the top of the building. PC Miles gained access to the roof 'through a fanlight'. And always, there was the melodramatic, as though the incident itself was not enough –

By this time the street below looked like a scene from a Hollywood gangster film . . . dozens of people living in nearby houses saw something which might have come out of a novel or film . . .

The *Croydon Times* of Saturday, 8 November, followed a similar line to that of the *Advertiser*, quoting demands for flogging made to Sir Herbert Williams, MP for East Croydon, and a similar appeal by the Venerable C. F. Tonks, quoted above, who read the address at Miles's funeral. There is a photograph of Pearl Ware, cuddling her pet tortoise beside a very impressive home-made tortoise house, complete with chimney and television aerial! The East Ward women, where Miles lived, passed a unanimous resolution at a meeting on the night of Thursday, 6 November:

* *Croydon Advertiser*

This meeting is greatly disturbed at the increasing number of crimes of violence in Croydon and many other parts of the country. It calls upon the Government immediately to take special measures to suppress such crimes, including the introduction of corporal punishment and severe penalties for the illegal possession of firearms or other weapons.

The inquest on Sidney George Miles was opened on Wednesday, 5 November, at the coroner's court. It was a court in which Miles himself had often given evidence on other cases and now his widow, pale but collected, stood in the same box. Catherine Miles, a brave lady to whom everyone's sympathy went out in that November, and to whom it should still go, read the oath in 'a quiet, steady voice'. When asked if she had identified her husband's body 'she just inclined her head'.

The coroner, Mr J. W. Bennett, said to the jury of nine men: 'You have been called in connection with the death of PC Sidney George Miles, who served in the Metropolitan Police Force in this borough and who, according to the reports I have received, was carrying out his duties last Sunday evening when he met his death from a gunshot wound in the head.'

Because the case was already *sub judice* in fact (the hearing having taken place on the Monday) Bennett merely took formal evidence of identity and cause of death. To this end, Dr David Haler, the local pathologist, agreed that the cause of death was a gunshot wound. The same Dr Haler was quoted in this and other local papers as saying that the recent death of a man on the operating table of the Mayday hospital was a 'shocking piece of bad luck'.

The ubiquitous DCI Smith was there, as was Inspector F. G. Piper, Z Division's Welfare Officer.

John Parris has his own views on all this:

Coroner's inquisitions, when a trial is pending, serve no useful purpose, and, in the circumstances of this case, to require Mrs Miles to identify her husband's body and then speak of it in public was an agony which she might well have been spared. The only result was to increase public indignation against the two accused, and possibly prevent them receiving an impartial trial.*

* Parris op. cit.

We must do what the jury at the Old Bailey was unable to do. We must ignore the nonsense garbled to a greater or lesser degree by the Press. Thirty-seven years on, this ought to be easier, but as will emerge in the next chapter, the truth with the passage of time has a new enemy, more powerful even than contemporary prejudices. It is the conspiracy of silence which settles on the scene. And it is evident in the ignored letter, the unreturned phone call, the closed file . . .

On 5 December 1952 a portentous event took place which would have delighted Shakespeare and his groundlings. If it wasn't exactly lions whelping in the streets, it was a twentieth-century equivalent. It was the start of four days of the worst London smog in recorded history. Then it was seen as no more than an inconvenience; now it is described by Steve Elsworth in his book *Acid Rain* as one of the worst peacetime catastrophes the country has ever witnessed. Technically, what happened was that an atmospheric inversion developed over London – a layer of bitterly cold air trapped the rising smoke of the still-Victorian city, leading to a massive build up of sulphur dioxide. Visibility was reduced to five yards; people collided with lamp posts and railings. For four days the metropolis was at a standstill. Buses and trains didn't run. The AA was swamped with calls from stranded motorists. The Smithfield Show was abandoned and the police patrolled gingerly, wearing life jackets and carrying hooks on poles for fishing people out of the Thames. Animals choked to death. At the end of the four days there were 4,000 dead, 2,000 hospital cases and countless numbers ill. Looking back, it seems astonishing, but at least it led to the Clean Air Act of 1956.

And while all this chaos was occurring, Frank Cassels, John Parris, Christmas Humphreys and J. S. Bass were limbering up for the 'trial of the century'.

The Central Criminal Court was established in 1834 for trying criminals in the London area, a district of some 420 square miles and including about six million people. In 1901, the present buildings were erected on the site of the notorious Newgate prison in the Old Bailey, and its famous gilded figure of Justice – blind indeed in 1952 – was fitted to the dome nine years later. The Bailey was badly damaged by enemy action during the war and Courts 1, 2 and 3 had been restored; a fifth court was opened only two months before the trial began. The authorities had taken the opportunity to improve the comfort of the fittings. Gone were the high, uncomfortable Dickensian desks and Counsel now sat on plush leather benches. A microphone network called witnesses from lobbies rather than the ludicrous 'echo' effect of a human chain calling from the court. Dining facilities and a crèche were available to witnesses and the jurors had their own self-contained accommodation with restaurant, cloakroom and retiring room. The trial of Christopher Craig and Derek Bentley was the opening of a very busy calendar, the busiest for four years. No fewer than 101 people stood trial in that session and the speed of the case (like that of John Christie in the following spring) has few parallels at our end of the twentieth century.

Despite the weather, the crowds were huge and 'black market' tickets for the spectators' gallery of No 2 court cost as much as £30, a substantial sum in 1952. The harassed Bentleys arrived on foot; the Craigs in a Rolls-Royce paid for by the *Sunday Pictorial*, poised on the eve of the era of cheque book journalism. Their man Harry Proctor was assigned to the Craigs to make sure that no rival papers got anywhere near them. And the sum at issue was said to be £350. Mr Craig, the old soldier, looked dignified and solemn. His wife had been crying. His daughter Lucy, black-haired and beautiful, made some of the crowd catch their breath.

John Parris also arrived on foot, struggling up Old Bailey from the bus stop with a bulky red bag and bulging briefcase. He had had two days to prepare, having been dumped with a pile of depositions and one sentence: 'Counsel will obtain all information he needs from the depositions enclosed herewith and conference with his client.'*

He had managed to wheedle out of Lord Goddard, the Lord Chief Justice of England, who was to preside at the trial, an adjournment until 9 December and he had to do this in the Lord Chief Justice's presence in London, necessitating the chartering of a private plane (by no means an easy feat in 1952) to get back to his current case in Leeds. Goddard himself had insisted on Parris's personal presence – and this, of course, from the judge who was so concerned about the wasting of professionals' time in the case of the medical witness later in the trial.

Parris had met Christopher Craig on the previous Saturday, in the interview room at Brixton Prison, and was quite astonished by him:

* Parris op. cit.

Looking at him, sitting quietly, bandaged up . . . it was difficult to picture him doing any of the things he had done. For the outstanding impression was one of femininity. He had dark brown eyes, soft, bow-shaped lips and a smooth skin that would have passed as attractive on any girl, and his voice and manner were diffident and gentle. Perhaps his appearance was a clue to his character; that he felt a need to constantly assert to himself his own masculinity by possessing guns and emulating those he instinctively felt to be more mannish characters and, ultimately, by deeds of cruelty and violence.

Parris knew the damage that image could have on the jury and disapproved of Craig's suede jacket, bright trousers and Crêpe-soled suede shoes. He told him he should turn up at the Bailey looking less like an American gangster: 'Well, see that your father buys some [clothes] for you before Tuesday – something quiet and conservative.'

At 10.30 on the morning of Thursday, 9 December, the trial began. Parris's introduction to the Bailey, where he was clearly an outsider, was not auspicious. On the previous Wednesday he walked in on Christmas Humphreys in a scene we would recognize from John Mortimer's 'Rumpole' – 'Oh! he's some young chap who hasn't been called long. I suppose he got the brief because he's related to the Croydon solicitor.' I hope the silence hurt. Parris was not, as far as he knew, related to the Croydon solicitors Parris and Co. and they certainly hadn't briefed him, then or ever. It was a firm of Croydon solicitors, John Stevens, who had briefed Cassels.

Parris was the new boy, the 'foreigner' as he called himself. No one spoke to him as he found a cramped corner of a table for his wig box.

The original jury was composed of ten men and two women, drawn from the ranks of ordinary citizens whose names appeared on the electoral roll. Parris challenged both women, for two reasons. First, the challenging of jurors has the effect of establishing the presence of the defence counsel and perhaps catching prosecution counsel off his guard. Second, he wanted no female emotion – 'Where there is a crime of violence, women become so blinded by their horror of the crime that even if they entertain doubts of the accused's guilt they give the benefit of the doubt to the prosecution. For with more vivid imaginations than men, they can see and feel it happening to *them*, and their minds, in this case, would have been with the widow of PC Miles.'* It is also

* Ibid

possible, of course, that women would have identified more readily with the sorrowing Mrs Craig than with the sorrowing Mrs Miles. But Parris was at the sharp end of this decision, more in tune perhaps with sympathetic responses than we are thirty-seven years later.

It is now time to consider more closely the role of the Lord Chief Justice in the Craig and Bentley case. Winston Churchill called him 'Lord God-damn' and Stanley Jackson in *The Old Bailey* (1978) described him as 'short, chunkily built and apparently compounded of granite and volcanic lava . . .' Lord Denning was impressed by the length of his imposing upper lip.

Like most of his colleagues in the legal profession of his day, Rayner Goddard had attended public school (Marlborough) and Oxford University (Trinity College). Like Christopher Craig, he was a good sportsman. Like Christopher Craig, he was a poor shot. He obtained his degree in the casual, laid back way expected of gentlemen in Victoria's England, where three years of Dining in Hall at Oxford were thought as important as written examinations. There is a curious parallel in the fact that he joined the Western Circuit, the very one presided over by Judge Jeffreys, whose 'bloody assize' had terrified and victimized the West Country in the 1680's. Fenton Bresler takes 328 pages to tell the story of Goddard. There can be no doubt that he was a larger than life figure, but I feel he is still waiting for a real biographer. And it is a pity that such an eminent and sensible man as Lord Denning should have been prevailed upon to write the foreword to Bresler's book. No doubt Goddard was a firm and steadfast friend. No doubt he had the agile mind and ability to seize on the vital ingredients of a case. No doubt he embodied the common law. And that he did not suffer fools gladly and stood no nonsense from anyone is the stuff of which authority is made. 'All respected him,' writes Denning, 'some feared him. None dared scorn him.'

But we are not concerned here with Rayner Goddard the man, but with Rayner Goddard the judge. With Rayner Goddard, the judge at the trial of Craig and Bentley. More, we are concerned with the fact that this particular judge was the Lord Chief Justice of England – a man of immense influence and power. If such a man were known to favour capital punishment – which Goddard was; if such a man were known to favour a return to the birch – which Goddard did; then he would carry millions with him. Stanley Jackson asserts that Goddard's reputation as a latter-day Jeffreys is unfair, but there is little in Goddard's legal career to justify the assertion. In 1948 he made his maiden speech in the Lords on the proposed Commons amendment to the Criminal Justice Bill, vigorously denouncing the experiment of suspending the death sentence for a trial period of five years. Even then, the duly elected representatives of the people were not prepared to delay sentence if in the course of a crime a policeman or prison officer were killed. The salutary truth, of course, is that Goddard spoke for the vast bulk of his fellow judges and of the legal profession when he talked of the need for hanging. 'In my humble opinion, there are many, many cases where the murderer should be destroyed': in this particular statement only two members of the Bench disagreed with him. And judging by the supportive letters in national and local papers at the time of Craig and Bentley, such as that of Canon Symon quoted above, we can be forgiven for thinking that no one other than Chuter Ede, the Labour Home Secretary, and a handful of MPs thought differently.

The fact that the majority of the legal profession – and probably of the country at large – took Goddard's anti cosh-boy stance does not excuse his lack of impartiality. It has little defence morally. It has no defence in law. And if anyone doubts that the Lord Chief Justice of England was more than a little partisan in No 2 Court of the Old Bailey in those foggy days of December, if anyone accepts the whitewashing of his biographers, let us look at the evidence.

On Bresler's own admission Goddard interrupted 250 times. A man's life hung in the balance in that court-room. And Goddard's balance was decidedly off. That the man's extraordinary bias was hardly ever challenged by defence counsel is a shocking indictment of the system, of Goddard's power and of their inability to cope or indifference to the plight of their defendants. This will be considered later. To be fair to the Lord Chief Justice, having read every word of his quoted in the trial transcript in the 'Notable British Trials' series, I can find only one hundred and four interruptions. Of these, sixty-five are spoken in terms of contempt for Craig and Bentley or are underscorings of prosecution points or questions designed to bail a prosecution witness out of difficulty. Thirty-seven are 'indifferent' points, where Goddard is merely asking for confirmation on a matter he had not entirely grasped. And two *could* be described as pro-defence. These last are so unusual, it is worth recording them so that the reader can judge how useful they were. The first was an attack on Sergeant Edward Roberts: 'Do you not remember without your notes, officer?' Apparently, Roberts could not. It seems to be a commonplace in criminal trials that the police do not refer to their notes. The logic of this escapes me. Even so, it was hardly an impressive blow to the prosecution's case. The second example is highly ambivalent. I have assumed it is an example of kindness because I cannot believe so honest a man as Lord Denning could have misread Lord Goddard so entirely. The Lord Chief Justice reminded the court at one point that Bentley was unable to read his statement. It depends, of course, on the tone of voice in which the line was delivered. It could equally have been another example of contempt.

Of course it is not the role of the judge to support the defence or to be kind to the defendants. But equally, it is not his role to assume the mantle of an extra prosecuting counsel. Rereading the transcript, I am left with the distinct impression that if Goddard felt that Humphreys or Bass had not driven home their point forcefully enough, he was on hand to help them out.

First, he showed impatience with defending counsel on several occasions. 'To what issue is this going?' he asked Parris when he was cross-examining Niven Craig.

'There is an issue if your Lordship will allow me.'

'Well,' replied Goddard, 'We must keep within some bounds.'

And again: 'The doctor [Jazwon] is here to give medical evidence, not speculate on the flight of bullets.'

'I was asking,' countered Parris, 'whether what he found, [Fairfax's] wound, is consistent with that theory.'

'That is a matter you can address the jury on. It is not a matter for the doctor.'

And yet again during Parris's examination of Craig: 'Let us get on to something that matters.'

It is of course the job of the judge to control a case in matters of law and of conduct, hence the gavel-pounding and 'I shall clear the court' so beloved of court-room drama writers, but in all honesty I can find nothing in the defence conducted by either Parris or Cassels which is anything but relevant and proper.

Second, Goddard was extremely supportive of the police even though on the evidence of the trial transcript their testimony had yawning holes in it. When Cassels smelt a rat in Fairfax's evidence –

'You see, I do not want to take advantage of any slip; but you did agree with my learned friend Mr Humphreys that Bentley broke away *after* the shot was fired; you said "Yes" to the question he asked?'

'If I did,' answered Fairfax rather lamely, 'I have made a mistake, because Bentley actually broke away from me *before* the shot was fired.'

'The witness is quite right,' Goddard leapt to the sergeant's defence, 'I have a note of it. "As we got to the bottom of the left-hand corner Bentley broke away and shouted 'Let him have it, Chris.' There was a shot, a flash and I felt something strike me."'

'I quite agree, my Lord,' persisted Cassels, 'but subsequently Mr Humphreys asked a question which was framed like this: "As a result of your being shot and knocked down did Bentley break away?" And the answer was "Yes" . . .'

Goddard made no reply to this. Had he not a note of this also? And again, when Bass was clarifying the position of McDonald on or off the drainpipe, Goddard sensed a loophole and plugged it with what must be one of the most blatant pieces of bias in judicial history –

'Was it minutes or seconds?' Bass asked, to ascertain PC McDonald's time in climbing down the pipe.

'Minutes,' replied McDonald.

'Minutes?' Goddard checked him.

'Well, a minute, my lord.'

'What had you got to do?'

'I had to find my foothold as I went down; but it was not long.'

'Do you think you could have counted sixty?'

'I am not sure that I could.'

So, by judicious angling, Goddard had reduced McDonald's 'minutes' to less than sixty seconds, but not content to leave it there, he underscored the whole point of his interruption –

'People can always say minutes when they mean seconds in these cases.'

Harrison needed help as well. Commenting on the variance of McDonald's testimony from his, Parris asked: 'If the officer McDonald says that at that time Craig was the other side of the stack, is that right or wrong?'

'Well,' suggested Harrison, 'from what I saw . . .'

'You need not tell us.' Goddard and the seventh cavalry thundered to his rescue. 'Whether one man is right or wrong . . . There can be comment afterwards if you differ from PC McDonald *if it is material.*' [My italics]

It *was* material. Goddard dashed it aside. Neither Parris nor Cassels reintroduced it. And it has taken thirty-seven years to surface again.

Third, the Lord Chief Justice disparaged the defence's attempts to query the peculiar forensic evidence, especially of the nature of Fairfax's wound. 'I very much regret,' said Goddard, 'that you [Dr Jazwon] have been brought all the way from Manchester. The procedure of binding over was introduced for the purpose of saving time of people who have been conditionally bound over. The wound you gave evidence about and the passing [of the bullet] across the skin could have been perfectly well read . . .'

So Goddard had already prevented Jazwon from 'speculating' on whether Fairfax's version of his wound was correct and he made it quite clear that this was not acceptable procedure. In other words, there must be no possibility in the minds of the jury that Craig's version of what happened was the correct one.

Generally speaking, Humphreys and Bass had very little to do in the case of Regina versus Craig and Bentley. The case appeared open and shut and the hinges were oiled by the experienced partisanship of the Lord Chief Justice. Every time he sensed that Parris or Cassels was about to make a salient point, he demolished it. The classic case, but it is by no means the only one, is that of Humphreys' re-examination of L. C. Nickolls, the ballistics expert. Lest the jury should consider that an inaccurate gun could cause death by misadventure, rather than premeditated murder, Goddard interrupted with –

'This revolver, if it is fired off, and even if it is fired indiscriminately, is quite capable of killing people?'

'Yes,' replied Nickolls, 'it is capable of being lethal.'

'No matter,' continued Goddard with his love of underlining a point for the benefit of the simple souls on the jury, 'whether it is accurate or inaccurate.'

But of course all Goddard's interruptions pale into insignificance beside his summing up. On the point of law on which the case hinged – that is, the issue of whether Craig *meant* to kill Miles – there is no doubt that he was correct. Whether the law itself has much to do with the innate concept of justice is another issue sadly beyond the scope of this book. But in terms of his interpretation of the law as it stood in 1952, Goddard could not be faulted. One gets the impression that Parris challenged his interpretation out of some desperation, but the Lord Chief Justice was not to be swayed. Remember that here was a man to whom words, precision tools in his profession, had a special significance. Especially in a summing up to a jury of ordinary, inexperienced laymen who had just been bombarded by two and a half days' evidence and powerful oratory arguing both sides of a case.

Especially in a case of murder when the death penalty was still in vogue. Not a particularly subtle use of language then, when he said:

'It may be – and indeed I think it is – probable that you will see that there is no room for manslaughter in this case. *However, it is a matter for you.*' [My italics]

It smacks too much of Mark Antony's verbal annihilation of the men who killed Caesar: 'For Brutus is an honourable man.' Goddard, in attempting to condense the facts, went off into such a reverie that those facts became garbled and an entire flight of fancy took place. Note again the emotive use of language:

> The very first shot that he [Craig] fired hit a police officer [Fairfax] ... [Fairfax] got up and ... the prisoner fired a second time. The other police officers were heard ... coming up the stairs and then the third shot was fired in the direction of the stairs and PC Miles fell dead. The aiming does not seem to have been bad, does it? – Three shots, two police officers hit, one fortunately slightly, the other hit between the eyes, *so that blood gushed out* [my italics] and he fell dead simultaneously.

Only then does Goddard say that Harrison was fired at in his position on the other roof. This sequence of events was of course inverted. Harrison was fired at *before* Miles and the shot which killed Miles was the fifth or sixth. Parris corrected the judge on this later, but by then I would suggest the damage had been done. Goddard was a powerful orator. He revelled in histrionics and Parris had no right in the protocol of an English court-room to stop him in mid-flow. Whose words were carried away to the jury room, I wonder, by the twelve men and true? Those of Parris, defending a remorseless young thug; or those of the berobed, omnipotent Lord Chief Justice of England? Interestingly, when Parris did correct him, Goddard's throw-away comment (the last the jury would have heard on the matter of the number of shots fired) was, 'I do not know that it matters much.'

It didn't matter to Lord Goddard because he had already made up his mind that Craig and Bentley were guilty. He may even have made it up before the trial started.

But the most extraordinary piece of jury-leading is evident in Goddard's histrionics with Craig's knuckleduster and Bentley's knife. He put the knuckleduster on, explaining to the jury what it was and how it worked – 'A dreadful weapon' – although its relevance to the case was limited. If Miles had been beaten to death with it, Goddard's behaviour might have been excusable. As it was, it was pure playing to the gallery. But Lord Goddard was too old for the male lead, even that of ageing juvenile. Yallop quotes a young lawyer present in the court, who remembers being astonished by Goddard's final outburst when the foreman of the jury, rather curiously, asked to take Fairfax's jacket and waistcoat to the room when they went to deliberate. In the cold print of the trial transcript, the judge's comment is innocuous enough:

'You will remember of course, gentlemen, you are not considering the wounding of Sergeant Fairfax. You are considering the death of PC Miles.'

It is the *way* in which this was delivered that compels attention and raises doubts. Fenton Bresler, anxious to redress any imbalance in Yallop's view of Goddard, makes great play of the fact that the young lawyer Yallop quotes, Anthony Samuelson, was very difficult to find. The implication is, I suspect, that Yallop made him up. But as Bresler admits, he eventually found him and his letter to Bresler is worth quoting in full:

You are right in thinking that I am the Anthony Samuelson referred to in David Yallop's book. The incident was so indelibly imprinted on my mind that when I heard Yallop was writing his book, I took the trouble to get into contact with him through his publisher. This is a thing that I have never done either before or since. I am not the type who pushes himself forward into controversial situations.

At the time I felt very strongly that, whether or not Bentley was guilty in law of murder, he was not seen to be getting a fair trial. I do not think it matters very greatly whether Goddard said 'Death' or 'Murder' and if the official transcript said 'death' then I would not question its accuracy. The thing which stuck in my craw (and has stayed there for two decades) was the injudicial and partisan manner in which Goddard said what he said; and the fact that he said it, not to the whole jury, but to less than half of them; in fact the stragglers who were bringing up the rear . . .*

Christmas Humphreys was not surprised by Goddard's playing with the knuckleduster and smashing it down forcefully on the Old Bailey

* Quoted in *Lord Goddard* by Fenton Bresler

woodwork. It was the sort of ploy he often used himself. The dent in the woodwork was there for years.

Anthony Samuelson concluded his letter to Bresler:

> I think I was only 22 or 23 years old at the time. With the perspective that one gets from growing older I am now inclined to think that a strong Lord Chief Justice during those post-war years was of great and lasting value to the country. I could not see it at the time, but what was at stake may have been the very existence of the Rule of Law as we had known it. Should one, then, accept that there were bound to be one or two casualties? I don't know.*

What a tragic indictment of the system! What finer epitaph could there be on Lord Goddard? And what better evidence to prove Yallop's point that Derek Bentley died for the sins of his generation – 'to encourage the others'?

No such criticism can be levelled at the prosecuting counsel, Humphreys and Bass. Theirs was a straightforward case and public sympathy was on their side. The sad truth of course is that the British public loves nothing better than the underdog. And the British press knows exactly how to champion such a cause. In November, the underdog was Sidney Miles, shot down in the prime of his life in the execution of his duty, 'so that the blood gushed out'. In January, the underdog was Derek Bentley, the 'three-quarter-witted lad' who had just gone to Croydon for the ride.

Christmas Travers Humphreys, described in his *Times* obituary in 1983 as 'gentle judge, eccentric and Buddhist', had been the Senior Prosecuting Counsel at the Bailey for nearly three years. His father was the famous judge Sir Travers Humphreys and his mother was a Justice of the Peace. The law, it seemed, ran in Humphreys' veins. He was a Malvern College and Cambridge man and in later life became the West's leading advocate of Buddhism, the author of many books on the subject. Perhaps it was his quest for inner peace which turned the forceful, vigorous prosecutor into such a lenient judge in later years. Curiously, Humphreys was involved as prosecutor in the three cases which did most to end capital punishment in this country – those of Derek Bentley, Timothy Evans and Ruth Ellis. More curiously still, it was the shocking fact of hanging a *woman*, albeit a guilty one, which counted for more than the hanging of two innocent *men*.

* Bresler op. cit.

John Stuart Bass is a rather more shadowy figure. By the time the 'Notable British Trials' book had been produced in 1954 by H. Montgomery Hyde, he was dead. His legal career at Lincoln's Inn had been disrupted by the war, but after demob with the rank of Honorary Major, he rapidly rose to work with Humphreys as First Junior Prosecuting Counsel at the Bailey by 1950. He was briefly an additional judge at the Mayor's and City of London Court in the months before his death.

The prosecution opened with reasonable clarity when Humphreys reminded the court, as did the defence later, that there had been a great deal of publicity concerning the case and that this should be ignored. For a man to whom oratory is bread and butter, Humphreys came out with some spectacular Irishisms. Fairfax, he said, in the final shoot-out with Craig 'ran straight at him in a semicircle' and 'These four men will be the four principal witnesses of what happened on the roof, except that one of them is now dead – Miles.'

Essentially Humphreys told the roof-top story as outlined in chapter one. His opening sentence was 'Now the story is this . . .' as though subconsciously he knew he was bending the facts. He and Bass then conducted their case, more or less alternating in the interrogations, calling twenty-four witnesses, seventeen of them policemen.

First came PC Charles Beard of Z Division who produced his roof-top plan, copies of which were available to the court. The roof was flat, covered in asphalt and it measured 90 feet long by 54 feet wide at the narrow end where Fairfax found Craig and Bentley. The broad end was not measured but it appears from the scale to be about 60 feet wide. The staircase head was measured and marked with a 'B'; the lift-shaft head, referred to throughout the trial as 'the stack', with an 'A'. Then came the police photographs by Chief Inspector Percy Law of the Yard's Photographic Department. He had taken five photographs in the weak November sunshine of the morning following the incident. The rain still lay in puddles from the previous night, washing away the blood of Sidney Miles. The most interesting photograph is the one taken from Fairfax's approximate position as he reached the roof, showing the stack as light-coloured and surely visible even on a dark night, with the sloping glass and asbestos roof beyond. The same photograph shows the door of the staircase head to be open, its pebbled glass window smashed. These photographs were to be widely reproduced in the press at the time of the trial.

Then, more poignant perhaps than anything else the Prosecution had up their sleeves, Niven Matthews Craig, ex-captain of the London Scottish, a hero of the Great War, who had the misfortune to be Christopher Craig's father, was called to the stand. His evidence was vital in pinpointing the age of his youngest son, to prove that he was old enough to be responsible in law for his actions. His other son, Niven Scott, was already serving time for armed robbery. Parris used the opportunity to establish that Christopher had been a good boy until recently. He had regularly attended Bible classes at Streatham, had a job at a filling station in Camberwell and had an ambition to be a gunsmith. His one failing was that he was dyslexic – that word had not been coined or made fashionable then; Craig senior called it 'word blindness' – and this made him a target for cruel class-mates and workmates.

'Was Christopher ever to your knowledge a violent boy?' Parris asked.

'Never,' Craig answered. 'He was in fact quite the opposite.'

'Gentle?' Parris persisted.

'Very gentle.'

Humphreys very properly could not let it go. He reminded the court under re-examination that both Craigs, father and son, had convictions for carrying firearms without a licence and that a large quantity of ammunition was found in the Craig house. Craig senior said he knew nothing of this.

Edith Ware, the witness whose daughter had first seen the intruders in Tamworth Road, gave her evidence next. Neither defence counsel cross-examined; after all, neither defendant denied attempting to break into the premises. This was really not the issue and there was nothing to be gained by such an implication.

The newly-promoted DS Fairfax had an altogether rougher ride. The essence of his testimony is set out in Chapter One, but both Parris and Cassels cross-examined him and elicited some confusion over the exact number of shots fired on the roof. It also became clear from the trial transcript that Fairfax had a ready ally in the Lord Chief Justice –

'The witness is quite right; I have a note of it.' And –

'Who was there to speak to? I do not understand.'

'Perhaps your Lordship will understand when the evidence of another police officer is given,' said a rather world-weary Mr Cassels. 'I am trying to check what this officer's recollection is of what took place.'

PC McDonald followed and the cross-examination made much of

the fact that his view of things was obscured by his having difficulty on the drainpipe at the time the crucial sentence, 'Let him have it, Chris', was uttered. There was a disparity between his testimony and that of Fairfax and later, Harrison, who swore that Craig fired *immediately* after the words were heard. McDonald had time to reach the ground during that 'immediately'. Once again, the Lord Chief Justice came to the defence of the beleaguered constabulary with his conversion of minutes to seconds on the drainpipe between Bentley's words and the shot.

Constable Harrison was sworn and under cross-examination it became clear that his testimony differed from both Fairfax's and McDonald's. He need not have worried – Goddard was on hand to plug the yawning holes in the police testimony. It was not Harrison's job to explain away such discrepancies. Not that is, until now.

Of the policemen on the roof, only Robert Jaggs, who arrived seconds after the death of Sidney Miles, was left alone by defence counsel. Neither Parris nor Cassels had any questions for him.

Sergeant Roberts, who took custody of Bentley and accompanied him on his ride to Croydon Police Station, was questioned in cross-examination about the prisoner's statements in the car, whether they were spontaneous or elicited by questions. Interestingly, the third policeman in the car, James Leslie Alderson, also of Z Division but stationed elsewhere, was not called as a witness. Christmas Humphreys, almost as an afterthought to Roberts, asked:

'And he is available if he is wanted, so far as you know, is he?'

Roberts's answer was 'Yes.'

Constables Stewart and Ross testified on the last seconds of Craig's stand on the roof, although oddly, their versions differed. One said that Craig was firing wildly into the air; the other that the gun was pointed directly at him. Doctor Nicholas Jazwon, who attended Sergeant Fairfax at Croydon General Hospital, was quizzed by the defence on the peculiar nature of his wound. There was no fracture of the collarbone and the bullet appeared to have travelled upwards, tearing a jagged hole in Fairfax's jacket before lodging in his braces behind his back. The bullet had fallen out during the examination. Again, the Lord Chief Justice saved the witness from any decision-making – 'The doctor is here to give medical evidence, not to speculate on the flight of bullets.'

Lord Goddard was sorry that Dr Jazwon had been brought 'all the way' from Manchester and was convinced that his expert testimony could just as easily have been read in his absence.

Another doctor, the pathologist David Haler, gave his views on the post-mortem findings on Sidney Miles and, perhaps rather to the disgust of later theorists of the case, neither defence counsel cross-examined him. The underlying assumption of the time was that Craig had shot Miles. It was the *nature* of the killing that was to be Parris's defence.

Lest defence should imply that Craig's comments while in the hospital were due to the influence of drugs administered, Dr Gordon Hatfield, who attended Craig, itemized the doses given and the exact times and dates. Much play was made by the defence that one of these drugs was Pentathol, the so called 'truth' drug. Hatfield was able to confirm, however, that nothing taken by Craig at Croydon general could 'affect the clarity of his mind to the extent that he did not understand what he was saying.' Neither were there any signs of concussion, which would presumably also cloud the judgement of the sufferer.

Sergeant Stanley Shepherd of Z Division was badgered by Frank Cassels to know exactly how the statement made by Bentley was delivered. It seemed – and seems on a rereading of it – to be disjointed, garbled, as though Bentley was replying to specific questions, rather than dictating in his own words. Although Cassels implied that there was nothing wrong with this technique, both Shepherd and DCI Smith denied emphatically that any questions had been asked. All Shepherd had done occasionally was to jog Bentley's memory by reading the last sentence he had dictated to him.

By four in the morning of Monday, 3 November, Detective Sergeant Stanley Shepherd and Detective Chief Inspector John Smith, both of Z Division, were taking a statement from Bentley. He had been cautioned (for the umpteenth time in fact since the adventure on the roof) which meant that in time-honoured tradition he had been warned that he need not say anything, but that anything he did say would be taken down in writing and might be used in evidence. In view of the fact that Bentley was now effectively facing a murder charge, it might be as well to hear that statement in full:

I have known Craig since I went to school. We were stopped by our parents going out together, but we still continued going out with each other – I mean we have not gone out together until tonight.

I was watching television tonight (2 November 1952) and between 8 p.m. and 9 p.m. Craig called for me. My mother answered the door and I heard her say that I was out. I had been out earlier to the pictures and got home just after 7 p.m.

A little later Norman Parsley and Frank Fazey called. I did not answer the door or speak to them. My mother told me they had called and I then ran out after them. I walked up the road with them to the paper shop where I saw Craig standing. We all talked together and then Norman Parsley and Frank Fazey left. Chris Craig and I then caught a bus to Croydon. We got off at West Croydon and then we walked down the road where the toilets are – I think it is Tamworth Road. When we came to the place where you found me, Chris looked in the window. There was a little iron gate at the side. Chris then jumped over and I followed. Chris then climbed up the drainpipe to the roof and I followed. Up to then Chris had not said anything. We both got out on to the flat roof at the top. Then someone in a corner on the opposite side shone a torch up towards us. Chris said, 'It's a copper. Hide behind here.' We hid behind a shelter arrangement on the roof. We were waiting for about ten minutes. I did not know he was going to use the gun.

A plain clothes man climbed up the drainpipe and on to the roof. The man said, 'I am a police officer. The place is surrounded.' He caught hold of me and as we walked away Chris fired. There was nobody else there at the time. The policeman and I then went round a corner by a door.

A little later the door opened and a policeman in uniform came out. Chris fired again and this policeman fell down. I could see that he was hurt as a lot of blood came from his forehead just above his nose. The policemen dragged him round the corner behind the brickwork entrance to the door. I remember I shouted something but I forget what it was. I could not see Chris when I shouted to him. He was behind a wall. I heard some more policemen behind the door and the policeman with me said, 'I do not think he has many more bullets left.' Chris shouted, 'Oh, yes I have,' and he fired again. I think I heard him fire three times altogether. The policemen then pushed me down the stairs and I did not see any more.

I knew we were going to break into the place. I did not know what we were going to get – just anything that was going. I did not have a gun and I did not know Chris had one until he shot. I now know that the policeman in uniform that was shot is dead.

I should have mentioned that after the plain clothes policeman got up the drainpipe and arrested me, another policeman in uniform followed and I heard someone call him 'Mac'. He was with us when the other policeman was moved.

There was one basic problem with this statement. Even though the method of taking a statement is that a policeman writes it (Sergeant Shepherd did so), it is then customary for the dictator of the statement to read it through himself before signing it. In this case, Derek Bentley was incapable of doing this. Like Craig, he could not read well enough. He signed it in three places, once for the written caution, once for the start and once for end of the statement itself, and had to ask Shepherd how to spell his own name. Even then he managed to leave an 'e' out of Derek. In an attempt to write 'This statement has been read to me and it is true' he could only manage 'Tis as Be' before Shepherd took over and did it for him.

Perhaps Cassels should have pushed harder. William and Iris Bentley were convinced there was nothing of the real Derek in these words. And his father's account of the events of November 2nd is at variance with it in a number of important details.

Next a series of constables – Denham, Smith, Sheppard and Brown – testified as to Craig's remarks while in his private room at the hospital.

Craig had been taken by ambulance to Croydon General, as had the wounded DC Fairfax, and both men were examined by casualty officers. Dr Gordon Hatfield attended Craig and found his injuries to be exactly as described by the specialist, Dr Douglas Freebody, at the trial:

He had a fracture of the seventh dorsal vertebra and a fracture dislocation of the manubrium sternum (which is the breastbone, in front of the chest) and also a fracture of the left wrist.

He was given no medication until the small hours and then only codeine compound to ease the considerable pain he must have been in. According to Craig himself, he drifted in and out of consciousness for some time and could not remember making comments to the succession of policemen ordered to observe him in his private room. According to Craig, the first thing he was aware of was someone hitting him in the mouth and calling him a murdering bastard. First to call was the overworked DS Shepherd, who arrived at about 11 p.m. on the night of the shooting.

'I had six in the gun,' Craig told him, 'I fired it at a policeman. I had six tommy gun bullets' . . . 'Is the copper dead?' he asked. 'How about the others? We ought to have shot them all.'

When DCI Smith arrived half an hour later, the conversation followed the same pattern.

'I have just seen the body of PC Miles in Mayday Mortuary,' Smith told him, 'and as the result of inquiry I have made I am charging you with being concerned with another man in murdering him.'

'He's dead, is he?' Craig asked, 'What about the others?'

DS Shepherd visited the Craigs' home in Norbury Court Road shortly after one o'clock that morning. In the boy's bed he found a .45 calibre bullet and hidden under the floorboards in the attic a piece of sawn off gun barrel and a tin box which contained the extraordinary arsenal of twenty-five rounds of airgun pellets, twenty-two rounds of .22 rifle ammunition, twenty-eight rounds of .32 revolver bullets, twelve rounds of .38 revolver bullets, forty-six rounds of .31 revolver bullets, three rounds of .45 revolver bullets, eight rounds of .303 rifle bullets and five rounds of .303 blanks.

Later that morning, PC Vincent Denham of Z Division, sitting beside Craig's bed in the hospital, heard him say, 'Is he dead? That copper. I shot him in the head and he went down like a ton of bricks.'

To PC Thomas Sheppard, Craig said, 'What do you get for carrying a knuckleduster? Bentley had mine.' . . . 'Did you see the gun I had? It was all on the wobble, so I took it to work and sawed two inches off the barrel.'

More damningly, to PC Ernest Brown on 6 November, Craig said, 'If I hadn't cut a bit off of the barrel of my gun I would probably have killed a lot more policemen. That night I was out to kill because I had so much hate inside me for what they did to my brother. I shot the policeman in the head with my .45. If it had been the .22 he might not have died.'

On the second day of the trial, Detective Chief Inspector John Smith of Z Division discussed the Bentley statement and the circumstances surrounding it as well as the nature of the forensic evidence – the finding of a number of spent cartridges and bullets on the roof and in the gun itself, which Craig had dropped in his headlong dive. For the first time, Cassels in cross-examination raised the issue of Bentley's intelligence.

'Do you agree with me that he is below average intelligence for his age?'

'Oh, yes.'

'Well below it?'

'Below it, sir. I cannot say well below it.'

Smith was quizzed as to the existence of bullet marks on the glass and asbestos roof behind the stack in a re-examination by Christmas Humphreys, anxious to tidy up any loose forensic ends. In a rare moment in this 'trial of the century', defence counsel accused the prosecution of leading his witness –

'. . . that is not what Fairfax said. He said when he fired Craig was in the corner on the east side.'

Mr Humphreys took the point like a gentlemen.

The Lord Chief Justice shrugged. 'I do not think it matters one way or another.'

Lewis Nickolls, Director of the Metropolitan Police Laboratory, New Scotland Yard, was the last prosecution witness. Parris cross-examined him closely and Humphreys examined and re-examined equally closely. Craig's gun, though in working order, was inaccurate, both because he had sawn off the barrel and because he was firing incompatible bullets. After a welter of calibre information which probably left the jurors, even those who had conceivably seen a high degree of active service, reeling, the Lord Chief Justice went for the jugular with his extraordinary grasp of the essential facts of a case:

'This revolver, if it is fired off and even if it is fired indiscriminately, is quite capable of killing people?'

'Yes,' replied Nickolls, 'it is capable of being lethal.'

But the bullet that killed Sidney Miles was never found. That single fact has given rise to extraordinary speculations and led David Yallop in 1971 to claim to have 'startling new facts' on the case.

What are we to make of the job done by the defending counsel, Parris and Cassels? Francis Henry Cassels, educated at Sedbergh and Corpus Christi, Cambridge, was called to the Bar of the Middle Temple in 1932. During the war he served as an officer in the Royal Artillery and was mentioned in dispatches in 1945. He was Deputy Chairman of the County of London Sessions and lived until his death in 1989 in Surrey. E. John Parris is more difficult to locate. Because of his disbarment over his involvement in a trading company, he does not appear in the conventional mini-biographies of great men. One current judge who knew him all those years ago was suspicious of him, in an affectionate sort of way, and astonished that he got on so well. He had the ability to bounce back from defeat and reversal, perhaps because he had the showman's knack of placing himself at the centre of any stage. Certainly, both men were labouring under immense difficulties. Parris in particular was given very little time to prepare, busy as he was with a case in Leeds. And if public sympathy backed Crown counsel, by definition it opposed the defence. This would not have mattered except that, as we have seen, public sympathy is reflected in the minds of the twelve members of the public whose duty it is to decide the verdict. However much all parties might insist on no trial by the media, this, I have suggested, was impossible.

Under the structure of English law, the essential thrust comes from the prosecution. And David Yallop is of course quite wrong when he implies that defence counsel normally now have the last word. They certainly speak after the prosecution's closing speech, but the impact of Parris and Cassels' rhetoric was seriously reduced, as we have seen, by the extraordinary partisan delivery of the judge.

There were times, certainly, when both Parris and Cassels missed opportunities to challenge witnesses, most obviously perhaps when they failed to cross-examine Dr David Haler, the pathologist, on the nature of the wound which killed Miles. This will be discussed below. Of the two, Parris was certainly the more fiery and beneath the careful words of the trial transcript, we can sense his rising annoyance with the old man on the Bench.

'I do not know why the doctor [Jazwon] has been brought from Manchester to say that,' said Goddard.

'I thought the jury might like to appreciate it,' replied Parris.

And later, with the same witness: 'If your Lordship will not allow me to ask the question, that is all.'

But Cassels showed his exasperation too. 'Perhaps your Lordship will understand,' he said, 'when the evidence of another police officer is given. I am trying to check what this officer's recollection is of what took place.'

The defence called Christopher Craig himself, who was allowed to sit down for the proceedings. Parris took him through the violent playground of South London, inquiring into his interest in guns, whether he was a good shot. Craig said he was not; he'd only been on one rifle range in his life and he was not impressive. He carried guns to school and to work and had owned over forty of them over the years. A rather pitiful picture emerged of a dyslexic boy who carried guns to impress his friends, the friends who mocked him because he could not read – 'It just made me feel big.'

All in all, Craig's defence was weak, but for a sixteen-year-old of limited ability he was able to score some surprising points over the articulate seventy-five-year-old judge, not to mention the fifty-one-year-old leading counsel for the prosecution.

'Are you saying,' asked Humphreys at one point, 'that you did not hear that?' [Bentley's remark 'Let him have it, Chris']

'Bentley did not say it, sir,' Craig replied.

'Three officers heard it in the darkness from different points of the compass.' Humphreys in full cry, hounded his man, 'Are you saying he did not say it?'

'I am saying I did not hear it and if they heard it, they have better ears than mine.'

On the subject of jumping off the roof, Lord Goddard interrupted, 'How do you know where you landed if you were unconscious?'

Craig replied, 'Because I am quite a good diver and I have been off a lot of heights.'

On the matter of any remorse Craig may have felt over the death of Sidney Miles, Goddard bludgeoned the defendant: 'You are asked whether you ever expressed any regret to anybody.

Craig replied, 'Who is there [in prison] to express it to, sir?'

Craig's testimony differed markedly from that of the police, but that was to be expected. He claimed he fired wildly, intending to frighten away the police. He explained that he had never intended to shoot anybody, let alone kill. His roof-top shouts were 'bluff' and bravado. He was only sixteen and although he never once admitted it, Christopher Craig was scared. As for his callous and ruthless statements from his hospital bed, he couldn't remember saying them. If he had said them, they were attributable to his being 'hardly conscious half the time.'

Like a grandfather past patience with a naughty grandson, Goddard interjected at this point, 'Hardly conscious! Don't talk such nonsense.'

Christopher Craig had killed one policeman and wounded another. It was not surprising that not one single policeman at Craig's bedside remembered the boy crying for his mother.

When Derek Bentley was sworn to give his testimony, the 'grandfather' whom Fenton Bresler has described as 'the greatest Lord Chief Justice of this century' showed his total lack of understanding of contemporary youth.

'Where were you going?' he asked.

'Just to Croydon, sir.'

'Yes, but what for?'

'Just for the ride, sir, an ordinary ride.'

Men of Lord Goddard's ability, standing and social background never went anywhere just for a ride. Men of Derek Bentley's ability, standing and social background didn't often do much else. Cassels made little of Bentley's limited intellect. He made little of the fact that the younger Craig had far more personality and that he easily dominated the relationship. The fact that Bentley remembered Craig from school and not the other way around bears witness to this fact. There is nothing of Bentley's being turned down for National Service on grounds of limited intelligence; nothing of his having been consistently demoted at work – first to road sweeper and eventually to unemployment. Cassels' line of defence had more to do with events on the Croydon roof-top.

Bentley said in court that he had not realized Craig intended to commit burglary until he hopped over the gate at Barlow and Parker's. He did not know Craig had a gun until Craig fired at Fairfax. He had been given the knuckleduster by Craig earlier, but he really didn't know why. The fact, of course, of which nothing was made at the trial, was that Fairfax had found the knuckleduster in Bentley's right pocket where Craig had put it. But Derek Bentley was left-handed. He had never even touched it. Above all, at no time did he say 'Let him have it, Chris,' or incite Craig to use his weapon. He had never offered any violence against the police and on the two or three occasions that he had had the opportunity to rejoin Craig by virtue of being left unattended, he had meekly remained where he was – where Fairfax had left him, in fact, sitting behind the staircase head. He had made no mention of the sort of gun that Craig was carrying. He couldn't tell one from another. He made no reference to the fact in the car on the way to Croydon police station. 'I did not think he'd use it. He's done one of your blokes in,' was the kernel of the police statement concerning this journey.

Christmas Humphreys summed up the gist of Bentley's evidence throughout: 'So that is four police officers – Fairfax, McDonald, Roberts and Stephens – whose evidence is untrue against your evidence which you say is true?'

'Yes, sir,' said Bentley.

I doubt if it impressed anyone.

Much was made of the relatively unimportant remark from Bentley on the roof: 'They're taking me down, Chris.' Bentley remembered saying something of the sort, but he wasn't sure exactly what. Asked why he had said this, his answer was logical enough:

'That was in case he shot me, sir.'

'You were only thinking of your own skin, you mean?' sneered Humphreys. The later inference the Prosecution drew from this remark was altogether more damning: that it was yet another incitement for Craig to save Bentley by firing his gun. Either way the 'three-quarter-witted boy' could not win. Reginald Paget in *Hanged and Innocent?* says that Bentley could not have made a fool of himself by his monosyllabic answers in court – God had done that for him already. Eyewitnesses in the court observed that as Bentley stood down, he looked totally shattered, 'like a zombie'.

The slur against Cassels, later a judge himself, is that he didn't care about Bentley and didn't try as hard as he might. Bresler, in his biography of Goddard, defends Cassels by saying that he battled on in defence of his client by taking the case to the Appeal Court. But this was a matter of course in murder trials, especially in the days of the death penalty. As we have seen, the appeal failed. It is unfortunate that Cassels's remark to John Parris when they met on the Monday before the opening of the trial – 'I think both little beggars ought to swing' – was reported by Parris in his book *Most of My Murders*. Bresler, the lawyer, the man on the inside, closes ranks to defend his colleague:

> . . . For it would be a bad day for the independence of the Bar and the quality of our justice if Counsel were only to represent causes with which privately they were in sympathy and persons for whom, as individuals, they had feelings of liking or affection.

December 11th 1952, the day that Craig and Bentley were found guilty, *was* a bad day, for them certainly, for society certainly and for the Bar too. For Bresler's glib statement needs comment. Of course it would be physically impossible in the real world for every counsel to admire and like his client. But to imply, as Bresler does, that a lawyer will give of his utmost in any cause on some abstract principle of justice or the rule of law is fantasy. A lawyer may be spurred by a cause – one thinks of Clarence Darrow's brilliant defence in the Tennessee Monkey Trial or his impassioned plea for mercy on behalf of the psychopathic Leopold and Loeb. More usually, he may be spurred by a fat fee – and this was certainly not the case for Parris and Cassels with Craig and Bentley, because they defended for a pittance under the Poor

Prisoners' Defence system. But can we *really* believe there is another *raison d'être*? As a teacher of sixteen years' experience, I know in my heart of hearts that I am guilty of similar attitudes. A child who does not like my subject, or a child who is difficult, does not engage my sympathy. I will not pull out all the stops for him or her as I would for someone else who loved history, who behaved and worked hard. I challenge any teacher to say they react differently. The same is true of barristers. Cassels admitted, in an interview with Anna Feuchtwang of the *Croydon Post* in June 1987, that he did say, 'I think both little bastards ought to swing.' (John Parris, either out of kindness to his colleague or in deference to his readers' sensibilities, gives the milder 'beggars'.) If he really meant it, then surely there is at least room for the question: how hard did he try?

While the jury retired for their lunch on that second day, 10 December, the Lord Chief Justice and the respective counsel argued an issue of law on which the case was to revolve. It was clear that Parris interpreted the law one way, his Lordship another. At one point, Lord Goddard said, 'I think this is a little too subtle for me.'

The closing speech by the Prosecution was infinitely better than the opening one. Humphreys seemed to have got over his 'Irishisms' and contended that the whole thing hinged on the case of Rex v. Appleby 1940.

> Where two persons engage in the commission of a crime with a common design of resisting by violence arrest by an officer of justice, they have a common design to do that which will amount to murder if the officer should be killed in consequence of resistance. If therefore, an officer of justice is killed in such circumstances, both persons are guilty of murder.

Against Craig, the case was cut and dried. Police witnesses had testified to the fact that Craig had shot DC Fairfax. He had also shot – and killed – PC Miles. Every word he uttered on the roof was of hatred and hostility. Every word he uttered in hospital followed the same vein. He intended to kill, he killed and he showed no remorse for doing so.

In the case of Bentley, Humphreys contended that the lad was a willing accomplice, that he knew perfectly well that Craig was armed and that his shout of 'Let him have it, Chris,' testified to by three policemen, was a clear incitement of his armed partner to violence. Bentley himself had been armed – with knife and knuckleduster. He may not have tried physically to rejoin Craig behind the stack when he had the opportunity to do so, but he remained with him mentally throughout. His shout, 'Look out, Chris, they're taking me down,' was a further incitement to the armed Craig to prevent this from happening by using his gun again – 'And the answer to that,' Humphreys said, 'is a shot in their direction.'

> And I must ask you, in accordance with the oath that you have taken, to return a verdict on this indictment of guilty of wilful murder against each of these two young men.

John Parris introduced an eloquence all his own into his final speech on behalf of Craig. He reminded the jury of the meaning of the oath they had taken on being sworn. They had soon to decide the case on the evidence; they had sworn not to decide it on the prejudices of media and pub gossip. And his words, echoing down the years, have a grim ring of truth to them:

> The tragedy of this trial is that Christopher Craig has become a symbol of wayward youth; the nation's uneasiness and anxiety about the state of their youth has become focused on him.

The jurors were not, said Parris, to convict Craig out of passion and hatred. Quoting the eighteenth-century revolutionary Tom Paine, he said: '"We must see that our enemies do not suffer injustice."'

For despite Parris's urgings that Craig was not the young thug depicted by a Press anxious to capitalize on a story – 'Look at his eyes, his mouth, and the way he speaks!' – he could not possibly have hoped to make much headway there. The prosecution's evidence was too convincing. He asked for a softening of the verdict – one of manslaughter rather than murder – in that Craig had no 'malice aforethought'; he had not intended to kill PC Miles. Parris reminded the court of Craig's inadequacy in terms of his dyslexia, of his fascination with firearms, his need to feel big in front of his friends and no doubt in front of the police too. And he touched a human chord perhaps when he said:

> Members of the Jury, . . . Think back to the days when you played games of cops and robbers . . . that was [Craig's] mental attitude that night, I submit to you.

And then Parris raised an interesting point. He underlined the flaws in the police case by his contention that whenever a policeman 'saw a flash and heard a bang in the dark he thought it was a shot that was *aimed* at *him*' [my italics], which explains the discrepancy between the statements of PCs Ross and Stewart. He reminded the jury that the 'silent witnesses' (examples of forensic evidence) testified if anything in Craig's favour. There was no evidence of a bullet mark on the chimney-stack where PC Harrison had been crouching. The wound on Sergeant Fairfax and the tear in his jacket suggested the ricochet of a bullet fired from several feet away bouncing off the ground before finding its target by chance. There was no bullet lodged in the doorframe behind Harrison although he claimed he heard it crunch there. And there *was* a bullet found in the bottom right-hand corner of the roof, in a position totally free of policemen, which bolstered Craig's contention that he fired over the roof-tops to frighten the policemen away. As for the death of Sidney Miles, '. . . you may conclude that it was a tragic, unfortunate, million to one shot . . .' in view of the acknowledged inaccuracy of Craig's gun.

Frank Cassels was no less eloquent in defence of Bentley and his task should have been all the easier in view of the fact that Bentley had 'come quietly' in the old police phrase, had not carried a gun and was actually under arrest at the time of the killing of PC Miles. Cassels too reminded the jury of certain conflicting remarks in police testimony as to what Bentley actually said. The only way, Cassels maintained, in which Bentley could be found guilty was '. . . if you are satisfied and sure, each one of you, a) that he knew Craig had a gun, and b) that he instigated or incited Craig to use it . . .'

In Cassels' view, these factors had not been proven by the prosecution.

At ten thirty on the following morning, Thursday 11 December, the Lord Chief Justice delivered his charge to the jury. Perhaps 1952 was too early. Perhaps the age of seventy-five was too late. For whatever reason, Goddard was not of the school to accept mitigating circumstances – 'Now let us put out of our minds in this case any question of films or comics, or literature of that sort.'

Goddard told the jury that it was their task to find for or against the defendants separately and he outlined the law with regard to the killing of a policeman:

... and the law for centuries ... has given special protection to police officers in the execution of their duty ... in the case of a police officer who is killed, the law does not give the accused the same defences as in the case of other persons.

And he went on to quote the case of Mr Justice Brett, later Lord Esher, who in Victorian times ruled that when a kick was aimed at a policeman by a man resisting arrest, and that kick subsequently caused death, it should be described as murder. A pity that the Lord Chief Justice's memory was at fault. The victim was not a policeman, but an innocent passer-by. But the law had not changed, and John Parris's eloquence was in vain because he had misread the law.

'"If a police officer has arrested"' quoted Lord Goddard, (not once but twice) '"or is endeavouring to arrest ... a person ... and that person, for the purpose of escaping, or of preventing or hindering the arrest, does a wilful act which causes the death of an officer, he is guilty of murder, whether or not he intended to kill or to do grievous bodily harm."'

To help the jury to a decision, Goddard clarified police evidence, even to the extent of condensing the time taken between shots (a point of fact on which Parris quite properly corrected him when he had finished), and he interpreted Craig's roof-top and later statements thus:

You may wonder why he said 'I am only sixteen.' Possibly you may know that the law does not allow a capital sentence to be passed on a boy of sixteen. Was it a boast? 'Ah ha! Come on! I've got a gun. I can't be hanged.' You will think of that.

In his reference to Bentley, the Lord Chief Justice asked for the lad's weapons to be put before him and he tried on the knuckleduster:

Have you seen a more horrible sort of weapon? . . . It is a shocking weapon . . . Here was Craig, armed with a revolver and that sheath knife . . . one wonders, really, what parents can be about in these days, allowing a boy of sixteen – they say, perhaps, they do not know, but why do not they know? – to have a weapon like this which he takes about with him . . .

When Parris corrected him on the number of shots fired, the prejudice of the judge was revealed in all its Establishment glory: 'It does not really seem to me to matter very much whether it was the third shot, or the fifth shot, or the sixth shot.'

Perhaps it was Parris's correction that had rankled, for when the Foreman of the Jury asked, before they retired to decide their verdict, to take Sergeant Fairfax's coat and waistcoat with them, Goddard burst out with astounding vehemence that the wounding of Sergeant Fairfax was not the issue. Delivered as it was to stragglers of the jury already filing out, it was an extraordinary and gratuitous outburst.

The twelve men and true took exactly seventy-five minutes to reach their verdict. At 12.30 p.m. they returned to court with the news that Craig was guilty of murder and Bentley likewise, but with a recommendation to mercy. Neither Craig nor Bentley had anything to say and the Lord Chief Justice passed sentence – the sentence of death which the boy's father heard through a haze of fear and numbing shock.

And for his family, 'there was to be no more peace of mind for them, only [weeks] of sleeplessness and tortured nerves. And tea, always tea, to keep us awake and long silences and sudden sobs and the fear of daylight.'

Christopher Craig, you are under nineteen, [Goddard went on] but in my judgement and evidently in the judgement of the jury, you are the more guilty of the two. Your heart was filled with hate and you murdered a policeman without thought of his wife, his family or himself; and never once have you expressed a word of sorrow for what you have done. I can only sentence you to be detained until Her Majesty's pleasure be known. I shall tell the Secretary of State when forwarding the recommendation of the jury in Bentley's case that in my opinion you are one of the most dangerous young criminals who has ever stood in that dock . . . Take him down.

They took Christopher Craig to begin what was to be a ten and a half year sentence at Wormwood Scrubs and other prisons. Meanwhile his family, courtesy of the *Sunday Pictorial*, drove off in the paper's Rolls, had dinner at a riverside inn at Wapping and stayed in the Angel Hotel, Shepperton, where Mr Craig was to pour out his heart to Harry

Proctor in an extraordinary jumble of journalese. Alan Ladd, the actor, was staying at the hotel and Mrs Craig got his autograph. Ladd's immortal *Shane* was not released until the following year. His film reputation rested icily on *This Gun For Hire*, in which he played a cheap psychopath, complete with belted raincoat, trilby and gun.

The Lord Chief Justice had praised the men of Z Division and had asked Fairfax, McDonald and Harrison to stand forward together with their Chief Inspector.

> The conduct of the men of the Z Division on this night in arresting these two desperate young criminals is worthy of the highest commendation and the thanks of the community are due to the police for their gallant conduct. They are all deserving of commendation; but I have asked these three officers in particular to stand forward as they showed such commendable courage on that night. It is no light thing to face a burglar or housebreaker in the dark when he is armed with a revolver and firing the way he did. I doubt not that all your comrades who were there that night would have shown exactly the same courage that you did; it so happened that you three officers were exposed to the worst of it, and had, therefore, I suppose in one way one may say, more opportunities of showing the courage and resolution that you did. The thanks of all law-abiding citizens ought to be tendered to you.

There was a feeling at the time, and since, that justice had miscarried because the 'more guilty of the two' – Craig – was allowed to live, whereas the less guilty – Bentley – was sentenced to die. The Lord Chief Justice had explained to the jury that just because he sat on the Bench and they in the jury box did not mean they had left their common sense at home. But that is exactly what the sentences in the Craig and Bentley case implied had happened. Not for the first or last time was it amply proved, in the immortal words of Mr Bumble, that the law was an ass.

Early in January the *London Gazette* carried the citations for the four policemen in the case:

> The QUEEN has been graciously pleased to make the undermentioned awards:

GEORGE CROSS

Frederick William FAIRFAX, Detective-Constable (now Sergeant) Metropolitan Police (Selsdon, Surrey).

Awarded the GEORGE MEDAL

Norman HARRISON, Police Constable, Metropolitan Police (Croydon, Surrey) James Christie MCDONALD, Police Constable, Metropolitan Police (Shirley, Surrey).

Awarded the BRITISH EMPIRE MEDAL (Civil Division)

Robert James William JAGGS, Police-Constable, Metropolitan Police (New Addington, Surrey)

A brief description of the roof-top 'adventure' followed, concluding: 'The Police Officers acted in the highest tradition of the Metropolitan Police and gave no thought to their own safety in their efforts to effect the arrest of armed and dangerous criminals.'*

When these citations were made public, an anonymous woman rang Sergeant Fairfax, taunting him about the value of the worthless George Cross. He immediately assumed that it was Lilian Bentley and rang her threateningly, demanding that the phone calls cease.

When distinguished people like Louis Blom-Cooper QC, Livia Gollancz, Lord Soper and H. Montgomery Hyde wrote to *The Times* in December 1971 with a demand similar to Yallop's that the case be reopened, the then Home Secretary, Reginald Maudling, made the following answer. He could not, he said, presume to retry the case. That was a job for the courts. His concern was 'to consider whether any fresh evidence has come to light which was not before the courts and which might have affected the verdict . . .'

In case Maudling were to be accused of doing a less-than-thorough job, he asked the Commissioner of the Metropolitan Police to make his own enquiries. From this it emerged that five pistols were issued to the police, each with eight rounds of ammunition, and that the only bullets fired came from Fairfax's .32 automatic.

Dr Haler could add nothing to his trial evidence. And neither, interestingly, could ex-DS Fairfax –

'Former Detective Constable Fairfax has also been seen and made a

* *Notable British Trials* op. cit.

statement in which he adheres entirely to the evidence which he gave at
the trial and to which there is nothing he is able to add.'

The Commissioner's verdict? –

In the light of these inquiries and of my study of all the facts, I have
found nothing to justify any action on my part in regard to the
conviction, or to warrant more extensive inquiries.

But the fact is that the Commissioner of the Metropolitan Police,
Reginald Maudling, W. G. Bentley, John Parris, even David Yallop,
were all looking in the wrong direction. Yallop comes nearest to the
right one when he says:

Three policemen, Pain, Bugden and Alderson, were all present at
vital moments. All in a position to confirm or contradict the
evidence of fellow officers. Evidence which, if accepted by the jury,
would hang Bentley. All three were missing from the witness box . . .
The absence of these three men constitutes one of the mysteries of
the case.*

Indeed it does. These 'three monkeys' who had 'heard nothing, seen
nothing, and now were saying nothing . . . simply melted into the
ranks of the policemen missing at the Craig/Bentley trial.'* *

One at least is missing no longer.

* Yallop op. cit.
* * Ibid

— 6 —

A GUNFIGHT IN THE DARK

Let me take you back. Back to November 2nd. The day the Italians call 'The Day of the Dead'. Police Constable Claude Pain spent the early part of that Sunday evening at a photography class at South Norwood. There wasn't enough time for him to get home before his shift started at 9.45 p.m. so he went in early to the old station in Fell Road. It had been raining and he was still wearing his galoshes when the phone call came through from John Ware. A routine call. There were intruders on the roof of Messrs Barlow and Parker, Wholesale Confectioners, in Tamworth Road. The call was taken by an operator, Dotty Kitchen, who passed it to Danny Watson, the station sergeant. Routine calls like this were answered routinely by whoever was on duty.

'Pain,' Watson called, 'are you ready? Get the van out. Suspects on the roof at premises at Tamworth Road.'

The man sitting with Pain in the station that night was Police Constable Allan Beecher-Brigden. He is Yallop's second 'monkey', but unaccountably Yallop refers to him consistently as 'Bugden', which may explain why he was unable to find him when he wrote *To Encourage the Others*. Allan Beecher-Brigden died in 1980, but his widow was kind enough to supply me with important corroborative material which makes nonsense of some assertions by various writers.

Contrary to Yallop's account, Pain and Beecher-Brigden first met Detective Constable Fairfax in the yard outside the station. He was not in the CID office. He was not typing up a report. And the 'one urgent word from Fairfax' to Norman Harrison — Yallop's histrionic 'buzz' — seems never to have been uttered. Far from Fairfax initiating the response to the call, he had to ask Pain what was going on as he (Fairfax) was returning a car to the station garage.

'What have you got?' Fairfax asked.

'Intruders on the roof at Tamworth Road,' Pain told him.

'Right,' said Fairfax, 'I'll hop in with you.'

There was no sign of PC Norman Harrison. Yallop's account is that Fairfax collected Harrison in the station yard as the constable was on his way to the staff canteen because he had forgotten to bring any sandwiches. Pain categorically denies Harrison's presence and Mrs Beecher-Brigden has never heard the name. Interestingly, Norman Harrison did not reply to Yallop's enquiries when he wrote *To Encourage the Others*. Fairfax and Harrison corroborate each other's story that they both arrived in the same van. But they corroborate other things too.

Beecher-Brigden normally drove a police car, one of those fitted with a two-way wireless to patrol the area and to arrive fast at trouble spots. His widow is of the opinion that he drove a car that night, but this seems not to be the case. All commentators on the incident as well as the trial evidence point to a van being used, probably because of the need to accommodate more than one intruder on the return trip to the station. The call was timed at 9.25 p.m. and by 9.29 the van had screeched to a halt outside the Barlow and Parker building in Tamworth Road. A minute or two later, a police car arrived. It was 7Z, driven by Sidney Miles. His wireless operator was James McDonald.

There was a small, excited crowd gathering at the front of the building and people were pointing and gesturing from upstairs windows. With the arrival of the police, Craig or Bentley or both began shouting and gesturing. If it was Harrison's torch beam which surprised them, he must have arrived by a different method altogether from the one he described at the trial. And if, as Yallop conjectures, Craig and Bentley hid silently behind the stack like ostriches with their heads in the sand, it was a belated and totally pointless ruse. Beecher-Brigden had already seen what looked like a gun in Craig's hand as he struggled out of his vehicle.

There seems to have been no concerted plan at all. Fairfax, arguably the senior officer present at this stage by virtue of his detective status, shinned up over the same gate Craig and Bentley had climbed minutes earlier. Pain did not see him do this and assumed in fact that Fairfax must have reached the roof from the back of the building. Beecher-Brigden stayed on the ground, so although his deposition was never used and he was not called to the hearing or the trial, his evidence can have no relevance to what happenned next on the roof. When the shooting started moments later, it confirmed his worst fears and he radioed the station to report that there were indeed two men on the roof and that one at least had a gun. He asked for reinforcements. And he asked for firearms. It was November 2nd. Bonfire night was only three days away. The station – probably Danny Watson on the other end of the line – laughed at Beecher-Brigden. It was kids letting off fireworks. He was told to have another look.

To make doubly sure, Beecher-Brigden did. By this time almost certainly, Fairfax had been wounded. Beecher-Brigden made sure with the second call that he was taken seriously. Here was a man on duty on a wet, dark night. His colleagues were unarmed on a roof in Croydon, facing bullets. It was his wedding anniversary. He was not panicking. And he was not mistaken. A rather shamefaced station sergeant promised reinforcements and firearms immediately. Beecher-Brigden was a large, heavy man. Acrobatics on drainpipes were not for him. He was of far more use on the ground.

• Claude Pain wasn't as sprightly as he had once been, either. Even so, he had to get to that roof. He rejected the six foot expanding gate over which Craig, Bentley and, unbeknown to him, Fairfax had climbed. Pain was a big man. He wasn't sure the gate would bear his weight and there seemed no obvious way up from there. In one of those quirky moments which no fiction editor would accept from a novelist, a resident from the other side of Tamworth Road came to his rescue.

'I've got an old ladder,' he said to Pain. 'It's up to you. If you want to risk going up there, you can.'

The ladder was a rickety contraption with at least two rungs missing, but to Pain it was heaven-sent. He hauled it upright against the front corner of the premises and climbed. It was short of the roof rim, but Pain was able to grab the rail that ran along it and pull himself up. As he jumped over the rail, he would have been a perfect target for Craig had Craig intended to shoot. Perhaps the boy was by this time behind the stack and out of sight. Pain estimates that he and Fairfax reached the roof at the same time, but for Pain to assume that Fairfax had climbed up from the back of the premises, he (Fairfax) must already have walked forward between the roof lights towards the stack. Before anything else happened, Pain was aware that the ladder – his lifeline – was being taken away from the wall by its owner! His immediate thought was how to get down in a hurry if he needed to. And that prospect seemed increasingly likely because the shooting suddenly started. Pain assumed the shots were being fired indiscriminately across the neighbouring gardens to frighten police and residents away (which in effect was Craig's testimony). He was armed only with a truncheon. Ironically, in the pocket of his police overcoat was his camera, fitted with flash and ready to use, which, had he thought of it, could have taken some of the most spectacular photographs of police action in existence and perhaps even ended the controversy of the Craig and Bentley case before it started.

Ahead of Pain stretched the roof – flat asphalt about the size of a tennis court. Directly in front of him was the brick wall of the staircase head. Slightly to his right stood the four roof-lights, like miniature greenhouses. He made for the staircase head first, crawling forward on his stomach. He nearly gashed his hand on sheets of glass which had been left lying around, presumably for repairs to the sloping roof beyond the stack. He reached the brick wall, but found his view impeded and so dashed across, a distance of some eight or nine feet, to the nearest of the roof-lights, the bottom left-hand one.

Let me take you back now to the evidence of the other policemen on the roof, those four gallant officers who never once mentioned the presence of Constable Pain.

Fairfax walked within six feet of Craig and Bentley, behind the stack as they were by this time. He shouted, 'I am a police officer. Come out from behind that stack.' Pain did not hear this. I suspect he was still negotiating the roof rail at this moment and there was considerable noise from people and sirens below. Neither did he hear Craig's alleged reply – 'If you want us, fucking come and get us!' – but Craig denied ever having said this and when David Yallop interviewed Fairfax in 1971, Fairfax, contrary to his trial evidence, denied it too.

Pain did, however, hear someone – and it had to be Fairfax at that moment – shout 'Keep your heads down. There's shooting! There's shooting!' This accords with Yallop's description:

> The sound of Bentley's voice jerked Fairfax back to life. Although the injury had been slight, he was suffering from a high degree of shock. He jumped to his feet, ran to the edge of the roof and shouted into the garden of Number 26, 'They've got guns! Get the place surrounded!' He ran to the front of the roof and again shouted down to his colleagues in Tamworth Road, 'They've got guns! Radio for more men!'

This presumably was when Beecher-Brigden made his second call.

It is noticeable that none of this emerges from Fairfax's testimony at the trial. According to that, his behaviour was that of a calm, collected and extraordinarily brave man. According to him, at this point he had been wounded in the right shoulder by Craig, which had caused him to lose his grip on Bentley. He had been knocked down by the bullet's impact and had then grabbed Bentley again. By this time, too, the fatal words had been uttered by Bentley: 'Let him have it, Chris.' As he grabbed Bentley a second time, Craig fired again and Fairfax dragged Bentley to the cover of a roof-light and frisked him, finding the knuckleduster and knife. They were now some fifteen feet in front of Pain and he would have been in a good position to hear everything that was discussed. Contrary to the rational picture of Bentley painted by Yallop –

He [Bentley] turned to Craig and simply said 'I'm going out . . .' As Fairfax fell to the ground Bentley ran to him and pulled back his jacket to examine the wound, asking 'Are you alright?'

– Pain remembers Bentley as hysterical and crying most of the time on the roof. When Pain first became aware of Bentley's presence it was as Fairfax grabbed him a second time. Fairfax was astride his man with Bentley pinned by his legs, pushing his face into the asphalt. It is worth reminding ourselves that *every* man on that roof was scared. Fairfax, Pain, Craig and Bentley. Given that situation, reckless statements are made. Silly things are said. I am perfectly satisfied that Derek Bentley was still babbling nonsense in the patrol car on his way to Croydon Police Station minutes later.

Pain was totally unaware of Norman Harrison's approach from the far chimney stack. Like other readers, he was confused by Harrison's testimony (which Pain saw for the first time in 1988) that he approached the stack on his back and it does take an effort of will to imagine the pitch of the glass and asbestos roof which made this necessary. Harrison could not have approached standing up because he would have slithered into the gutter and lost his balance. Had he approached lying on his front he would have had no view at all of events on the roof. Harrison says that Craig fired twice at him and then the policeman scuttled back to safety as fast as he could, anxious to find another angle of approach.

By this time Fairfax had thought better of the cover afforded by the roof-lights. Pain must have felt exposed here too, for the sides of the lights were only two feet three inches high. Fairfax had dragged Bentley accordingly to the better cover of the staircase head. It was now, on Fairfax's own admission, that Craig circled the roof in parallel with his friend and the detective until he reached the spot marked '90 ft' on the police plans submitted at the trial. From here, Craig had a clear shot at Fairfax, Pain and possibly even Harrison. *He did not fire* but went back to the stack again.

It was not until now that PC James McDonald finally reached the roof and only with the aid of Fairfax. He joined the two men behind the staircase head, eight or nine feet from the prone figure of Pain. McDonald recounts a conversation about Craig's gun of which Pain has no recollection:

> Fairfax said, 'He got me in the shoulder.' Bentley said, 'I told the silly bugger not to use it . . .'
> 'What kind of gun has he got, Fairy?' McDonald asked.
> 'It's a .45 Colt,' interrupted Bentley, 'and he has plenty of ammunition for it.'

One of the pieces of 'new evidence' which Craig submitted via his mother to Sir Frank Newsam at the Home Office in a last ditch bid to save Bentley was that he (Craig) said this, which corroborates Bentley's assertion that he didn't know one gun from another.

All the men on the roof now heard the commotion inside the staircase head. Fairfax takes up the story:

> The door marked 'B' [on police plans] burst open and officers called to me and I shouted back to them that I was round to their left.*

A thickset figure was silhouetted momentarily against the dim light of the stairs. He moved imperceptibly towards the stack and a shot rang out. The thickset figure instinctively raised his hands to his head before pitching forward on his face, eight or nine feet from Pain. Pain crawled forward into the open space and saw to his horror the three darts protruding from the back pocket of the prone policeman. He knew before he turned him over that it was his 'old mate', the keen sportsman, the darts fanatic, Sidney Miles. 'He must have been rushing up those stairs,' Pain told me. 'His blood must have been pumping. He looked like a pig.' Pain was to remember all his life that massive head, swollen with the bullet's impact, and the blood.

---

* *Notable British Trials* op. cit.

Together, the policemen dragged Miles's body to safety as Harrison leapt out of the doorway, throwing everything he could lay his hands on at Craig, who once again fired back.

Fairfax, McDonald, Harrison and Bentley, with the body of Miles, were now joined by PC Robert Jaggs. Pain had returned to the roof-light. The decision was made now to take Bentley down the staircase. The evidence of all the policemen on the roof at the trial was that they assisted in taking Bentley down. Fairfax went first, leading the way down the concrete steps. Then Bentley, pushed by Harrison, McDonald and Jaggs. All of them, for safety's sake, were actually *inside* the staircase head. Whether they *all* accompanied Bentley to the bottom of the stairs is not clear. When I was researching this book and talking over with my wife the logistics of the gun battle on the roof, it occurred to us that to leave the body of a comrade, even in an emergency, is not something that most men would do. To my astonishment, my eight-year-old son who had been following the conversation said, 'But Miles wasn't alone on the roof. Mr Pain was with him.' From the mouths of babes . . . Pain stayed with the body of Sidney Miles until Fairfax returned with his gun.

The last seconds on the roof appeared to have been a concerted advance on all fronts, led by the only man with a firearm. Fairfax, McDonald, Harrison, Jaggs and Pain all rushed the top left-hand corner of the roof simultaneously and Craig, out of ammunition, whether attempting suicide or not, threw himself over the rail.

Claude Pain helped the ambulance men carry the body of Sidney Miles down the steep stairs up which he had rushed minutes earlier. On the ground, among the hundreds of policemen, the ambulances, the fire engines, the crowds, he saw Sergeant Edward Roberts sitting in a patrol car holding a revolver in his hand.

'That doesn't look very nice, does it?' Pain said. It was a service revolver, painted khaki.

'You'd better make your way to the station,' said Roberts.

Which is precisely what Pain did. He made notes in his pocket book. He copied them up on the official form in longhand – the deposition that was never used; the deposition that disappeared.

Pain's link with the case had not quite finished. Along with other policemen, he was detailed to maintain surveillance at Craig's bedside in Croydon General Hospital in case he said anything. During the hours that Pain was there, all the boy did was to make odd little spitting motions out of the corner of his mouth. He said nothing at all.

The crux of the Craig and Bentley case rests on what happened in those twenty or twenty-five minutes on that roof-top in Croydon. Nowhere can it be better illustrated how in moments of panic and stress it is difficult, perhaps even impossible, for each second to be accounted for. But that is precisely what we must try to do. Because it was not done, Derek Bentley died. And the loophole of course, the excuse, was provided by the Lord Chief Justice himself during the trial:

> I wonder how anybody could be expected to be accurate on a matter like this [the exact number of shots fired] on a night like this when these men are being fired at, in fear of their lives . . .

In which case, m'lud, the whole prosecution case falls apart. If terror can blur facts and fear distort the truth, then there can be no case to answer. Case dismissed. But the case was not dismissed.

Parris saw his opening while cross-examining PC McDonald:

'As his Lordship says, it is rather unnerving to hear shots on a roof-top.'

'It is, sir,' McDonald assured him.

'It rather disturbs one's recollection of what happened?'

McDonald sensed the attack, the ground shifting beneath him: 'I do not know about that,' he said.

In the case of Craig and Bentley the sole evidence for the murder of PC Miles comes from four men, four men who were honoured and decorated for their heroism: Fairfax, Harrison, McDonald and Jaggs. In his introduction to the 'Notable British Trials' series H. Montgomery Hyde, MP, a barrister of the Middle Temple, wrote:

> Sometimes with a lesser crime when the accused challenges the accuracy and the veracity of the police evidence, the jury give him the benefit of the doubt. But it would be very difficult if not impossible to believe that . . . responsible police officers should have deliberately fabricated their evidence in a capital trial.

A previous reader has ringed this page (no. 16) and has written in pencil in block capitals in the margin against this text 'HA HA HA!?'

Let us take the police evidence in the case as it appeared in the trial, beginning with that of Frederick Fairfax. That he travelled with Norman Harrison to Tamworth Road has been called into question. It is hardly an earth-shattering point if it is untrue, but where there is one falsehood, there are likely to be others – 'The lie circumstantial . . . the lie direct.'

Fairfax's trial testimony, that he called upon Craig and Bentley to come out from behind the stack and that Craig's reply was 'If you want us, fucking come and get us,' was denied by Craig and has since been denied by Fairfax. The fatal words 'Let him have it, Chris,' were heard by Fairfax, Harrison and McDonald, but not by Craig, Bentley and Pain, even though Fairfax says they were shouted. 'That would *have* to have been shouted,' Pain agrees, 'and I did not hear it. I did not hear it because it was never said.'

And so we come to the vexed question of Fairfax's wound. David Yallop finds it odd – and worthy of official enquiry – that the *Police Review* of 7 November states that Fairfax had fired *before* he was hit. He concludes this because everything else in the article is correct and the *Review* got its information from a direct police source. This is not strictly true. The article talks in terms of Miles reaching the roof via a fanlight [*sic* – the same mistake was printed in the *Daily Express*, for example] and says 'he was shot as soon as he put his head above the roof' [*sic*]. Whatever the source of this article, then, it was clearly garbled. Brian Hilliard, the current editor of *Police Review*, explained to me that the journal was not essentially a reporting one then, but confined itself largely to comment. Given this situation, I see nothing sinister in what is merely another piece of misreporting.

Fairfax was under the impression that he was hit by a bullet from Craig's gun immediately after Bentley (in his testimony) had shouted, 'Let him have it, Chris.' There was some confusion between Fairfax, Cassels and Goddard as to whether Bentley had broken free seconds before, simultaneously with, or seconds after the shot. Cassels made the valid comment that the tear in Fairfax's jacket was a jagged one, not consistent with the neat round hole made by a bullet fired point blank. The findings of Dr Jazwon, Casualty Officer at Croydon General on the night in question, were that Fairfax had a slight wound in his right shoulder, that there was no bullet in the flesh and no fracture of any bone. He agreed on cross-examination by Parris that the bullet had been travelling *upwards* at the time of impact and had seared or scored the skin before coming to rest behind Fairfax's braces. When he undressed to be examined, the bullet fell out. When Parris pressed his man further, however, as to whether the wound could have been caused by a ricochet, Lord Goddard made the celebrated interruption referred to above, ruling in effect that Jazwon was not expert enough to make that judgement. The doctor was happy, I suspect, to be let off the judicial hook.

'Well, are you competent to answer such a question?' asked Goddard.

'No, I think not really.'

'You prefer not?' Parris put a different gloss on it.

'I prefer not,' the doctor said.

Had Jazwon – or a ballistics expert like Nickolls – been called upon to answer that question, or if Goddard had not intervened, there is no doubt that the resulting opinion in the jury's minds would have been very different from the one placed there by Fairfax's evidence. He said he had been no more than six feet away from Craig when he fired. And even ill-fitting ammunition from an inaccurate gun would have shattered his shoulder blade or drilled a neat hole. Even had it grazed the skin, the bullet's velocity would have carried it through the shoulder pad of Fairfax's jacket and on into the night air. The irrefutable forensics spoke for themselves. From Jazwon's testimony it is clear that the searing wound (or graze) was at the *front* of Fairfax's shoulder and the bullet had lodged in his braces. In other words, the 'silent witnesses' of forensics, of which Parris spoke at the trial, prove conclusively Craig's testimony, that he fired from some thirty feet away, not six, and that he fired at the ground, not directly at Fairfax, in order to scare him away. Unfortunately, the bullet had ricocheted off the asphalt and grazed the detective's shoulder. Indeed, the wound was so slight that Fairfax was to be seen, in the days after the incident, surreptitiously slipping off his sling in order to hand-crank an old car that he owned.

There is no mention in Fairfax's testimony of his rushing around the roof to warn colleagues on the ground. He was not, it is true, specifically asked to give that evidence. Perhaps he thought it was irrelevant. But if so, what else did he think was irrelevant? What else did he omit? Apart, that is, from the presence of PC Pain? He certainly remembered the conversation with McDonald about the sort of gun which Craig had got – a conversation which neither Bentley nor Pain remembered. And he remembered dragging Miles to safety, helped by PC McDonald. We will come back to Detective Sergeant Fairfax later.

Harrison's evidence is more straightforward. True, there is confusion over how he got to Tamworth Road, but because his first sortie was a solitary one, coming over the roof-tops from Numbers 25 and

26, his testimony is difficult to corroborate; particularly difficult, in fact, in terms of forensic evidence. Harrison says that Craig fired twice at him. The first bullet hit the asbestos roof somewhere behind Harrison. The second hit the chimney stack from which he was edging along the sloping roof. Inspector Smith, who investigated the scene of the crime in the watery sunshine of Monday, 3 November, found what *could* have been a bullet mark on the sloping roof near the 'g' of 'glass' on the police plan. But there was no sign at all of any bullet mark on the chimney. The prosecution had leapt in with an innacurate leading question to seal off that line of escape by the defence, by implying that the bullet mark on the roof was caused by one of the two shots fired by Fairfax as he ran towards Craig for the final shoot-out. Parris's counter argument, that it was miles wide of Craig's position in the top left-hand corner of the roof, is not strong. By all accounts, Fairfax was running in a semicircle, firing as he went. In that situation in the dark, his bullet could really have gone anywhere.

It is from Harrison that we have confirmation of Fairfax's version of events, or very nearly so. He heard Bentley shout 'Let him have it, Chris,' and was adamant at the trial that Craig fired two shots, one of which wounded Fairfax, *immediately* after this. He was less sure of other points. It seemed to him that Fairfax was taking Bentley to the staircase head before the shooting started. This does not conform with Fairfax, who says he was returning to collar Craig. And Harrison seemed curiously unable to point out the exact spot where Fairfax was standing at this moment:

'I am perfectly sure in my mind, but I cannot just quite describe it on here [the police plan].'

How odd.

How odd too that when Norman Harrison came rushing out of the staircase head door seconds behind the fallen Miles, he made no mention of PC Pain, crouching behind the roof-light directly ahead of him, eight or nine feet away, illuminated by the weak light from the stairs. Admittedly, he literally had his hands full, lobbing truncheon, milk bottle and block of wood at Craig, and admittedly he was in direct line of fire from Craig's gun. Alone of the policemen on the roof, Harrison remembered that after Bentley's 'They're taking me down, Chris,' Craig called out, 'Are they hurting you, Derek?' Yet another anomaly. Yet another unsubstantiated piece of testimony. David Yallop goes further. He doubts whether Harrison was on the roof at all in time to see Fairfax shot and to hear the fatal 'Let him have it, Chris.'

Harrison said he asked Fairfax if he was all right seconds before the phrase and that Fairfax replied. Fairfax does not mention this at all. And David Yallop had one huge advantage over more recent writers and that is that the premises of Messrs Barlow and Parker were still standing in 1971 when he wrote *To Encourage the Others* and he was able to walk around that roof-top and check eye-lines and distances. If Fairfax's testimony is correct, then the lift head would have obscured Harrison's view of what was happening between Fairfax, Bentley and Craig. That is not apparent, however, from the police plan and the police plan, in the absence of a correctly angled or panoramic photograph, is all the jury had to go on. This confusion might have been cleared up, of course, had Harrison consented to be interviewed by Yallop. He refused.

If there is confusion and conflict in the testimonies of Fairfax and Harrison, then McDonald's story multiplies the problem. His robust frame made negotiation of the drainpipe difficult. And because of this, it is by no means clear where he was when he claimed to hear the shout, 'Let him have it, Chris.' It seems likely that he was hanging on the highest section, with his head either level with or just below the roof, and that he was on the same drainpipe that Fairfax had climbed moments earlier. He was therefore some fifty feet away from Craig, Bentley and Fairfax, approximately the same distance away as PC Pain, who was crawling towards the roof-lights at this stage. In fact, the first thing that McDonald should have seen when he reached the roof was Claude Pain. Because McDonald could not see on to the roof at this point, he was unable to corroborate Fairfax's and Harrison's statements that Bentley had shouted 'Let him have it, Chris,' but he swore he heard *someone* say it. It is this discrepancy which led John Parris in *Most of My Murders* to postulate a third miscreant on the roof. There is, of course, a simpler alternative. Here, McDonald's and Harrison's testimonies part company, for whereas Harrison swore that Craig fired *immediately* after 'Let him have it, Chris,' whoever said it, McDonald had time to reach the ground again before the two shots were fired. We have seen already that the judge intervened to rescue McDonald on this point, converting by more than overt suggestion McDonald's 'minutes' to 'seconds'. If the defence could have established that *minutes* elapsed between 'Let him have it, Chris,' and Craig's shots, then the notion of Bentley inciting Craig to shoot Fairfax loses some of its credibility. Apart from the fact that Fairfax's wound was so slight he was now able to haul a heavy man over the roof rail; apart from the fact that Bentley stood or sat meekly by the staircase head while this operation was going on. McDonald now positioned himself with Fairfax and Bentley and the conversation about the gun took place, during which Bentley said, 'I told the silly bugger not to use it' – a conversation about ten or twelve feet away from Claude Pain, who did not hear it. But the most damning thing about McDonald's testimony is that he alone of the police on the roof categorically stated that he and Fairfax were the only policemen there. Cassels asked him:

'So far as you know, there were three people on the roof?'

'Yes,' replied McDonald.

'There was Sergeant Fairfax and the two men?'

'Yes,' replied McDonald.

And ironically, Cassels was to compound the villainy through his own ignorance – an ignorance not of his making, but based on a chronic injustice in the legal system which will be examined later. When Cassels was examining Bentley, he said:

'Now, do you remember when the first police officer, apart from Sergeant Fairfax, came over the rail?'

'Yes,' replied Bentley, 'I have forgotten his name now.'

'Never mind about his name,' steamrollered Cassels, 'it was McDonald . . .'

Equally, it could have been Pain. How was Bentley expected to know the difference? And how was Cassels expected to know that there was in fact a choice of constables?

Like Harrison, Constable James Christie McDonald declined to talk to Yallop when he wrote his book. And now he is dead.

The testimony of Robert Jaggs serves to spread the cloak of confusion. Fairfax does not mention him at all and it is clear that he got to the roof appreciably after the others. There is no mention in his evidence as to how he got to Tamworth Road or the time of his arrival. Indeed, in the trial transcript I have read he does not even state his rank or division. He climbed a drainpipe to the roof by which time Sidney Miles was dead. He saw the body, he saw Fairfax and McDonald holding Bentley. He saw Harrison. And a few feet from them, he should have seen Claude Pain. But of course he makes no mention of this in his court testimony. He crouched with Fairfax, Bentley and McDonald behind the staircase head and from time to time popped his head out. Each time he did this, shots were fired. It was he who heard more conversation from Craig than anyone else on the roof –

'Come on, you brave coppers. Think of your wives.' And –

'Come on, copper. Let's have it out.' And again –

'Give my love to . . .' as Craig leapt from the roof. Constable Robert Jaggs did not hear anyone say 'Let him have it, Chris,' because he was not in position on the rooftop by then. Neither did he consent to an interview with Yallop in 1971. And rumour has it that he drank himself to death in Balham High Road in 1978.

Who killed Sidney Miles? I must confess that when I began to write this book, I was intrigued by David Yallop's suggestion that it was not Craig's bullet, but a wild shot fired by the police themselves that ended his life; a view shared by the Bentley family. Having examined all the evidence available to me, I cannot find anything to support this view. I am going entirely on forensic evidence, because I find some of the testimony of Fairfax, McDonald, Harrison and Jaggs suspect. And if you dislodge one card, the whole house collapses.

Yallop's contention is that Miles was killed by an accidental shot fired by a police marksman somewhere on the roof of the warehouse between the chimney stack and the houses of Nos 25 and 26, Tamworth Road – in other words from the initial direction of Harrison's approach to the flat roof. Claude Pain remembers that that roof was very unsafe and the dramatized version on BBC Television in 1972 with its police thundering all over it carrying high powered rifles is pure fiction. In order to make the police shooting of Miles more plausible, Yallop tries hard to extend the time of the incident to upwards of forty minutes, in other words twice the time estimated by those on the roof. There is no reason to assume that this is correct, but it strengthens the view that a police marksman could have been present by giving him more time to get into position and to fire the fatal shot.

The official answer to the question of how many firearms were issued to the police was five. Firearms in London streets in 1952 were still, as we have seen, a rarity and despite the notion of something akin to a gun law mentality emerging, respectable society in that year was stunned by the roof-top incident. With the increasing availability and use of firearms in the 1970's and 80's the police have been forced closer to an American situation of training ever more men as marksmen and to act in such specialist capacities in sieges and hijacks. In 1952 no such training was given and the shock and surprise felt at the Fell Road Station by men expecting only fireworks is difficult for us to imagine. The man who issued the firearms was apparently Danny Watson, the station sergeant, although he would have had to have cleared this with a higher authority. I would assume that the khaki painted revolver seen in Roberts's hand by Claude Pain was one of those in question. When Yallop wrote, Croydon police station was unable to help on the number or type of guns issued. I put this question to the widow of Allan Beecher-Brigden. She believes that the only firearms issued were revolvers and that there were no more than three or four. Every officer issued with a weapon had to sign a chit for it and the number of rounds of ammunition with which he was issued. I also put the question to Claude Pain, who had no idea who was issued with guns but it was always, he said, a CID matter. Uniformed men were *never* issued with them. As far as he was aware, although he admits it was hearsay, the largest calibre bullet carried by police was .32; in other words the calibre fired by Frederick Fairfax. Apart from Fairfax, according to Mrs Beecher-Brigden, no other officers fired rounds; they had to account for any missing bullets when they returned their weapons after the incident. Finally Claude Pain remembers seeing no one at all on the roof behind Nos 25 and 26 where such a trigger-happy marksman would have had to be positioned in order to hit Miles.

What of the wound itself? First, the pathologist's report taken from his deposition made on 17 November:

There were two wounds in his head. One was at the inner side of the left eyebrow and was a typical wound of entry of a large calibre bullet. The other, slightly to the right at the back of the head, was the wound of exit of the same bullet. Death would have been virtually instantaneous.

In court Dr David Haler said substantially the same thing:

There were two wounds in the head; there was one immediately above the left eyebrow and the other one was at the back of the head, fifteen degrees over the mid line and running almost horizontally through the head and leaving the head in about *this* position [indicating].

The talk of two wounds is at first confusing. It should be understood that we are talking of a *single* shot, *one* bullet which hit Miles just above the left eyebrow near the bridge of his nose and exited at the back of the right side of his head. Anyone conversant with bullets and their impacts will know that the entry wound of such a bullet is usually a round hole a little smaller than that of the bullet's diameter. At that stage the conoidal bullet is tearing through skin and flesh and tissue and, in the case of the head, bone and brain at an indeterminate speed. To quote Gaute and Odell in *Murder: Whatdunit*:

> The natural elasticity of the skin closes [the wound] up slightly after it has been perforated and in doing so wipes the bullet clean. Entry wounds therefore have a circular bruise at their margin and also a grease ring. When the bullet strikes at an oblique angle [which was the case for Miles] the entry wound is more oval in shape and there is an irregular area of bruising. The blood loss from entry wounds is usually slight.

As for the exit wound:

> If the bullet has been deflected by hitting bone, splinters of bone and bullet fragments will lead to severe damage, causing gaping wounds as the debris is driven out of the body by the force of the shot . . . It is the practice of pathologists examining the victims of fatal gunshot wounds to pass probes through the points of entry and exit to establish each bullet track.

Neither Cassels nor Parris cross-examined Haler on his testimony, which astounded Yallop nineteen years later. Why? The only reason for Haler to have been cross-examined by the defence is if they had had an inkling that there was something suspicious concerning Miles's death – in other words, if they thought for one moment that someone else could have fired the fatal shot. But at that stage, the only person on the roof with a gun was Christopher Craig. It could not have been anyone else.

Yallop interviewed Haler in 1971 and says of that interview:

> He had privately formed the opinion that the wound could have been caused by a bullet of a calibre between .32 and .38. Craig was firing a .455 Eley. If Dr Haler's estimate of calibre is right then either Craig shot PC Miles between the eyes, firing a .38 bullet from a .455 gun (which a ballistics expert showed me was impossible) at thirty nine feet in the dark, or Craig did not fire the fatal shot.

Haler vehemently denied the implication that he withheld evidence at the Old Bailey, to the extent of threatening to sue both David Yallop and the *Guardian*, which carried Yallop's theory in an article. Both backed down, surely doubting the strength of their assertion. There is no doubt in my mind that as far as Miles's wounds are concerned, there is nothing to make us doubt that Craig killed him. Perhaps we would all have felt a little more secure on that point, however, if the pathologist in the case had been a Francis Camps or a Keith Simpson.

What of the bullet which killed Miles? It is clear from the trial that it was never found. Haler's view as expressed in the rather controversial interview with Yallop is that a bullet travelling through a head would still have the momentum to keep going for fifty yards. What is much more difficult to determine is in which direction it would go.

DCI Smith gave evidence at the trial on the number of spent cartridges and bullet marks found on the roof and its environs. Three were found to the west of the lift shaft (the top left-hand corner of the roof where Craig finally jumped over); four were still in the .455 Eley which Craig carried and which was found in the glasshouse below the roof; which meant that at least seven shots had been fired. Although he seemed anxious to protect Harrison's testimony, Smith was forced to concede that he found no bullet mark on either the chimney stack or the doorframe through which Miles and Harrison had rushed.

The ballistics expert was Lewis Nickolls, director of the Police Laboratory attached to Scotland Yard. Humphreys asked him:

'On the 13th November, 1952, did you receive from Chief Inspector Smith a .45 Colt revolver, exhibit Number 6 and part of a revolver barrel, Exhibit Number 7?'

'I did.'*

The gun may have been a .45 Colt to the impressionable, gangster-ridden Craig and Bentley, but to an expert like Nickolls, it was actually a .455 Eley and he was at pains to correct Humphreys on this. Both Humphreys and the judge were anxious to prove that although Craig's ammunition was not of the right calibre and that the gun's reliability was reduced by the fact that he had sawn off the barrel and sight, the gun was capable of killing. What they proved of course was that it *could* have been the fatal weapon, not that it was.

Exhibit Number 8, billed by Parris 'in all probability the fatal bullet', was found near the staircase head. It was distorted as though having undergone collision with something, but as it carried no traces of blood, Nickolls concluded it was probably not the fatal bullet. He

* *Notable British Trials* op. cit.

testified that the gun was inaccurate to a degree of six feet at a range of 39 feet (the estimated distance between Craig and Miles). Even so, one could have wished for a Robert Churchill.

What are we left with? I believe from my researches that it is possible that two men were responsible for the death of Sidney Miles. The first is Christopher Craig. There is no doubt in my mind that Craig fired the fatal shot, but equally I believe that he intended, as he claimed, to frighten away the police, not to kill them. Why else, when he had the chance, did he not shoot Fairfax and Pain when he had a clear view of them from his temporary position at the 90 foot mark on the police plan? How else can we possibly explain the extraordinarily slight wounds sustained by Fairfax? Just as Craig's first shot was a ricochet one, wounding the sergeant by accident, so probably was the fatal one that killed Miles. DCI Smith admitted that his forensic search of the roof-top was not as detailed as it might have been. My contention is that Christopher Craig was scared witless that night. Unlike Bentley, who whimpered and cowered and made irrational statements, the younger boy showed it by bluff and bravado. He screamed his hatred of the police, firing indiscriminately; over the roof-tops towards Harrison, whom he told Yallop later he thought was a fireman; on to the ground to drive Fairfax back, and vaguely at the centre of activity near the staircase head. Craig was not a good shot, but unfortunately the position of Miles's wound – 'between the eyes' – is associated in the public mind with expert marksmanship. I believe this was a tragic accident – that Craig's bullet found a mark for which it was never intended.

What is even more tragic is that Craig may have been unwittingly aided and abetted in the death of Sidney Miles by the very man who was the hero of the hour – Detective Sergeant Frederick Fairfax. When Yallop interviewed Craig for his book, he was told:

'What I've never been able to understand is how I shot him between the eyes when he was facing away from me and was going the other way.'

Claude Pain had similar difficulty reconciling this one. There are two possibilities. Either Miles was in the act of turning right to join Fairfax, but with his head turned – as would surely be natural – in Craig's direction. Or Fairfax made a very basic mistake. Let us examine his evidence again. In a desposition dated 17 November Fairfax says:

At this stage the door of the staircase head burst open and I heard officers call to me. I told them I was round to their right and that the fellow with the gun was round to their left.

So far, all quite logical and proper. But now look at his testimony in court:

'Is the next thing you remember then,' Humphreys asked him, 'the officers arriving within the staircase head?'
'Yes,' said Fairfax.
'What happened?'
'The door marked B [on the police plan] burst open and officers called to me and I shouted back to them that I was round to their *left*.'*

In that one careless misdirection, Fairfax was sending Sidney Miles straight into the path of Craig's bullet, whether it ricocheted or not. For Fairfax, along with McDonald and Bentley, was crouching behind the brick wall of the staircase head, to Miles's *right*, not to his left. It is astonishing that no other commentator has noticed this. Assuming that the trial transcript is correct on this point, there can be no other explanation. The line of Craig's bullet hit Miles's head at a point to suggest that he was turning left – in accordance with Fairfax's instructions – when the impact occurred. Only this can explain the entry wound at the front and the exit wound at the back. Miles had never seen this roof-top, presumably, until the second he died. All he had to go on was Fairfax's verbal instruction from beyond a closed door. That instruction was perhaps fatally wrong. Fairfax was under intense pressure on the Croydon rooftop. Like anyone in the witness box, he was under intense pressure in Number 2 Court of the Bailey. Did he *actually* say 'left' when he meant 'right'? I believe he did. Sidney Miles was not an idiot. Neither did he have a death wish. In turning left to face Craig, he believed he was turning to join his colleagues.

Two men died in that 'gunfight in the dark' – one there on the roof; the other three months later. To say that neither of them should have done is a trite and moralistic platitude. Sidney Miles died because he had the misfortune to be in the wrong place at the wrong time. So did Derek Bentley.

* *Notable British Trials* op. cit.

——7——
THE CONSPIRACY OF SILENCE

When I first came across John Parris's theory of a third boy on the Croydon roof-top, I imagined that he had invented him as a possible solution to the problem over the crucial words from Bentley – 'Let him have it, Chris'. On reading his *Most of My Murders*, however, it is clear that this boy is real enough, although whether he *was* actually present on the roof at that precise moment and whether he spoke the words is less certain.

Parris's contention is that when Norman Parsley and Frank Fazey came to call for Derek Bentley that Sunday in November 1952, it was with the intention of breaking into a butcher's shop in the London Road, Croydon, the keys to the safe of which Bentley had stolen the day before.

It is worth pausing to compare this line of thought with the day's events remembered by William Bentley, particularly with a bearing on Derek's statement to the police.

Craig had called, according to *My Son's Execution*, at the Bentleys' house just before lunch. Derek talked to him at the door because he was aware of his parents' attitude towards the boy. Little Denis, despite being told to go away, loitered in the passageway and heard Derek say:

'I don't want anything to do with it. Leave me alone.'

When William Bentley arrived from the garden, Derek clammed up, but he was white and shaking, as he had been on earlier occasions because of Craig.

'It's nothing, Dad, it's nothing. The bloke's barmy.'

There was silence over lunch. Iris went to work at 4.30 and Derek left for the same destination about 5.00 to see Betty Grable in *The Lady From The West*. He was back by 7.20 with a severe headache and had been unable to watch the pictures because of it. The boy had two boiled eggs, 'lashings of bread and butter' and a slice of cake of which he was particularly fond for what was to be his last meal at home.

He then settled down to watch the Old Time Music Hall, 'The Passing Show', on television. It was during this, between eight and nine, that Craig called for a second time. Lilian Bentley answered the door, and thoroughly unnerved by his behaviour with the knuckle-duster earlier in the day, told him that Derek was out.

'I always want you to tell him that, Mum,' Derek said, 'I know you will, Dad. I never want to see him again . . .'

Within fifteen minutes, there was another ring on the doorbell. It was the 'college boy', Norman Parsley, come to ask Derek out for a walk.

'He's all right, Mum,' Derek assured her. 'He's a good bloke.'

William Bentley went to the door to check and fell for it: 'I am a working man and I was impressed. I felt a sudden pride that a boy of his class should want to make a friend of Derek. If I had slammed the door in his face, Derek would not have gone to the scaffold.'

Derek Bentley's claim in his statement to the police is that Norman Parsley *and* Frank Fazey called on him, but William Bentley is adamant that Parsley was alone, even to the extent of stating that he looked up and down Fairview Road, presumably in search of Craig. He saw no one. It is certain, however, that both Fazey and Craig joined Bentley and Parsley once they were out of sight of the house.

Parris's claim is that there was a fifth boy with the group and that they made their way to the butcher's by about 8.00 p.m. They discovered that the shop was occupied, probably by the butcher doing his books, and decided, on Craig's suggestion, to tackle the Barlow and Parker warehouse in the belief that there was money stored there over the weekend. Claude Pain says that there was also a rumour that the upper storey of the building doubled as a jeweller's storehouse. According to Yallop, the gang toyed with the idea of breaking into an electrical shop first, but the presence of a courting couple prevented them.

At what point the gang of five became the gang of two – or was it three – is uncertain. The generally held view is that Craig and Bentley caught the 109 bus to Croydon alone. Parris implies that all five boys got there. By the time Mrs Ware looked out of her bedroom window, Parris maintains, there were three boys present. The assumption was made that the two she saw acting suspiciously outside the Barlow and Parker gate were Craig and Bentley. In fact, says Parris, they were

Bentley and A. N. Other, Craig having already scrambled over the gate to reconnoitre. And two pieces of evidence from the Bentleys support this. Mrs Ware was adamant that the figure everyone assumed to be Derek Bentley was pulling his hat down over his eyes as vehicles drove past him. But Derek did not take a hat that night. Iris told me he was very proud of his waves. His comment in court – 'I was always messing about with my hat, sir,' – applied to skylarking at home for the family's benefit. It did not explain his behaviour in Tamworth Road. Along with his coat, the trilby Bentley owned remained for the months and years ahead on the bed in the room which had become a shrine.

Secondly, Bentley had great difficulty with heights. Even standing on a chair made him dizzy and disoriented. Iris herself had given him three phenobarbitone tablets for his headache. She believes he could not have climbed the drainpipe without help. And Christopher Craig was surely not strong enough to do that without the help of a third party.

'It would be unfair at present,' says Parris tantalizingly, 'to disclose the name of the third youth who was on the roof-top that night when Fairfax and the other officers . . . got there, or to give details from which he could be identified; but he should take warning that if he continues to boast about it, as he is at present doing, he may yet find himself in the dock on a capital charge.'

Parris claims that the third boy made his escape over the glass and asbestos roof at the rear of the premises while Craig kept the police busy with his revolver. From where does Parris get his theory? Not apparently from his client, Christopher Craig, but from one newspaper account and some rather literal reading of Bentley's testimony.

The *Star* carried a stop-press column item on the night of Monday, 3 November:

Police are looking for a third youth believed to be on the roof of Messrs. Barlow and Parker's premises when PC Miles was shot.*

Parris makes the assumption that this *must* have come from a police source of some kind. It may well have done and it would be interesting to know the evidence on which the source was based as no other mention of the fact exists in the trial transcript or press reports that I have read. And even if it is correct, it by no means confirms the presence of the third boy. For months during the hunt for Yorkshire-

* Parris op. cit.

man Peter Sutcliffe in the Yorkshire Ripper enquiry, West Yorkshire police were looking for a Geordie, solely on the evidence of a hoaxer's tape.

The second piece of 'evidence' for the existence of the third boy comes from Bentley's garbled statement to the police where he says:

> A plainclothesman [Fairfax] climbed up the drainpipe and on to the roof. The man said, 'I am a police officer. The place is surrounded.' He caught hold of me and as we walked away Chris fired. There was nobody else there at the time. The policeman and I then went round a corner by a door.

It is that 'There was nobody else there at the time' which gave Parris food for thought. It *could* mean certainly that Bentley was referring to the fact that A. N. Other had by this time skedaddled over the roof into Upper Drayton Place. It could also mean that Bentley was referring to the fact that Fairfax's 'The place is surrounded' was incorrect; in other words, this was a ploy to make Craig and Bentley believe that resistance was useless. Had Bentley looked closely at this point to his left, he would have seen Harrison beginning his approach from the chimney stack; had he looked ahead, he would have seen Pain climb over the roof rail and begin to cross the roof towards him. Even if he had, it hardly constituted 'surrounded'. Equally likely, Bentley's remark was the kind of *non sequitur* which his father would readily have understood.

Bentley's statement to the police requires some further discussion. We have already established that it was elicited in a less-than-exemplary manner by tired, upset policemen in the early hours of the morning after one of their colleagues had been killed. Deny it though they might, DCI Smith and DS Shepherd have failed to convince me that they asked no questions of the frightened and confused Derek Bentley and that the statement was all his own words. In the early stages of writing this book my wife and I made statements to the police on a totally unrelated matter. My statement was written virtually verbatim, but when my wife used the phrase 'the van sped away', the constable, perhaps finding 'sped' archaic, wrote 'the van moved off at speed'. In this instance, it hardly matters in that the same meaning is conveyed. But the principle stands. Statements *to* the police should not be made *by* the police themselves. My wife could look after herself. She has an IQ, measured by Mensa, of 159 and she was not facing a murder charge.

William Bentley recognized his son in only the first two lines of the statement:

> . . . even at the best of times [Derek's mind] was foggy and confused; the simplest ideas baffled him. And four o'clock in the morning, in the emotional turmoil that followed the terrible events on the roof, was not the best of times. It was the worst conceivable time.

So Derek did not refer to Craig as 'Chris', but 'Kid' or 'Kiddo'. With his lack of intellect, if the police had referred to the other boy as Chris, Bentley would probably have done so as well. Fazey did not call at Bentley's house as the statement says. Derek did not run out after him, but took his time putting on his coat. And phrases like 'I should have mentioned' were beyond him. So we are at liberty to ask the question: whose statement is this? Derek Bentley's or that of Detective Chief Inspector Smith and Detective Sergeant Shepherd?

And if Parris can read things into this perplexing statement, so can I. As will be evident by now, the presence of PC Pain was awkward. If Smith and Shepherd knew of it, any reference to it had to be removed. So could not 'there was nobody else there at the time' be an answer elicited from Bentley to remove Pain from the scene? And his after-thought, the one that rang so false to his father:

> I should have mentioned that after the plain-clothes policeman [Fairfax] got up the drainpipe and arrested me, another policeman in uniform followed and I heard someone call him 'Mac'. He was with me when the other policeman [Miles] was moved.

Who called McDonald 'Mac'? If it was Fairfax, why didn't Bentley say so? He had already heard Fairfax speak several times. And why bother to mention so trivial a fact at all, if it were not in somebody's interest to specify *which* constable was present? By focusing on the uniformed 'Mac', we are in less danger of stumbling on to the uniformed Pain in Bentley's account of what happened.

Two things predominantly emerge from the case about the person-alities of Craig and Bentley. The first is that Bentley was of very limited intellect. If the police really suspected the presence of a third boy on the roof, can we really imagine that Bentley could consistently lie success-fully enough to fool them? The second is that Craig was a disordered, unpleasant and dangerous young man. Can we really accept that he would have such a high code of honour as not to divulge the third boy's name let alone his presence?

And why should the police in the trial make no mention of a third boy? Harrison in particular, dark night though it was, would have seen a figure retreating over the roof-top. And Constables Stewart and Ross, from that side of the building later found no safe way up to the roof. So how could A.N. Other find a way down to the ground?

Parris makes the point that Bentley only ever referred to Craig as 'Kid' or 'Kiddo', echoing William Bentley, so it must have been someone else who said 'Let him have it, Chris.' Yallop says – and does not quote his source – that this is incorrect: Bentley called Craig 'Kid', 'Kiddo' and 'Chris' indiscriminately. Parris also believes that Bentley told his parents the day before his execution of the presence of the third boy. If this was so, why did Mr Bentley do nothing about it? He was a tireless campaigner on the part of his son and always had been. He was a desperate man and had already gone to the Home Office days earlier with 'new evidence' from Mrs Craig which was not in fact new at all and carried no weight with Maxwell-Fyfe. If Bentley had told his father of the boy's presence, would this not have been the cause of yet another last-ditch attempt to secure a reprieve or at least a delay of execution? W. G. Bentley made no such attempt; neither does he mention it in *My Son's Execution*.

Was the third boy Norman Parsley? Was he Frank Fazey? Was he born out of Parris's intellectual problem of trying to explain away the discrepancy between the statements of the police and of Craig and Bentley? He certainly made no mention of a third boy at the trial itself, and in 1960 when he wrote his book was not prepared to name names.

But that is a limb along which Parris need not have crawled. His first surmise is the correct one:

> 'Let him have it, Chris,'; either [this was] a deliberate and wicked fabrication by police officers who, nobody will dispute, exhibited conspicuous courage that night, or [it] must have been used by Bentley. Of course, courage is not the same virtue as truthfulness and many a brave man might be a liar, especially if his emotions were lacerated by the murder of a companion for whom he had affection and knew that the killer himself was bound to escape with his life.

Parris is sailing into the waters of confrontation here. And because of the legal system as it stood in 1952, he was sailing in the dark. Unlike now, the police presented depositions, evidence and witnesses for the prosecution as they saw fit. That information was supplied to the counsel for the prosecution and the judge. It was not supplied to the defence. In other words, neither Parris nor Cassels, nor their respective solicitors acting on behalf of Craig and Bentley, had any evidence respecting the testimony of PC Pain. The nearest Parris comes to it, ironically, is with reference to another angle of the case entirely: 'Justice obviously demands that all eye-witnesses to material facts in issue should be called by the prosecution.' Correct. But the reader will by now be aware that justice had very little to do with the Craig and Bentley case.

The attitude of the police in general can be summed up by the anonymous officer who said loudly in the presence of Mrs Craig and Christopher when Niven Scott Craig was sentenced for robbery: 'Well – we've got rid of that bugger for a bit.' – and the attitude of most of the policemen on the roof in particular by Sergeant Fairfax's comment to Fenton Bresler in 1975: 'I suppose at the time my attitude was "That's one of them out of the way and it's a pity we couldn't have them both."'*

But how could the police be sure of getting either of them? Parris maintains that the law quoted by Goddard to the jury in the case – that both Craig *and* Bentley were guilty of *murder* in the shooting of PC Miles – is unclear. And he implies that it was Goddard's insistence on his (obsolete) version that brought in the guilty verdict. Craig was too young to hang. According to some police statements he had said so himself on the roof – 'I am Craig. You've just given my brother twelve years. Come on you coppers. I'm only sixteen.' – which left Bentley as the only legitimate target of reprisal for the death of Sidney Miles. But Bentley carried no gun. He had not fired one. He was technically under arrest at the time Miles was shot and had put up no resistance whatever to the police. Neither did he attempt to rejoin Craig or even try to escape, though he twice had the opportunity to do so. That did not leave much leeway to a vengeful police force who had just seen a colleague die in front of them. What was necessary in lieu of anything approximating to forensic evidence in the scientific sense, was a cast-iron statement, made by Bentley, which implied incitement to

* Bresler op. cit.

Craig to fire. That statement was the crucial, vital factor on which Derek Bentley was hanged. It was 'Let him have it, Chris.'

The statement itself bears some discussion. For Yallop, 'the phrase has indeed become a classic example, frequently quoted, to show the ambiguity of our language.' But there is no ambiguity. For the phrase to be ambiguous – for there to be any doubt as to whether it meant 'Hand over the gun. It's all over' or 'Shoot the policeman' – there had to have been discussion about the gun beforehand. Harrison says neither boy said anything prior to 'Let him have it, Chris.' Fairfax says Craig said, 'If you want us, fucking come and get us', though he later denied it. Either way, there is no talk of guns to make the phrase make sense. But doubly, there is no ambiguity, because the phrase was never used. Just as Bentley did not have the intellect to lie his way successfully out of any enquiry into the presence of a third boy, so he could not have defended himself against superior policemen and prosecuting counsel who tried to pressurize him into admitting he had said 'Let him have it, Chris.' I am convinced that if Bentley had said it, at some point he would have admitted it, either directly or having been tricked into it by skilful cross-examination of the type of which Christmas Humphreys was perfectly capable. But Derek Bentley denied having said it. Christopher Craig denied having heard it. And so too, more materially, did Claude Pain.

'As we got to the corner of the stack, that is the bottom left-hand corner of the stack marked "A" [on the police plan],' said Fairfax, 'Bentley broke away from me and as he did so he shouted, "Let him have it, Chris." There was then a flash and a loud report . . .'*

Fairfax was adamant that Bentley said it. So was Harrison – 'and as he did so the prisoner [Bentley] pulled away from him, broke away, and I heard him call out, "Let him have it, Chris" . . . Immediately afterwards I heard two shots fired from the direction of the lift shaft and I saw Sergeant Fairfax spin round and drop on to the roof.'**

McDonald doesn't *quite* conform – 'I heard someone shout "Let him have it, Chris."'*** – and on oath he could not swear it was Derek Bentley who had said it.

Jaggs was not on the roof at that time, so in that sense his testimony is irrelevant.

* *Notable British Trials* op. cit.
** Ibid
*** Ibid

And so we have the age old discrepancy between the police 'story' and that of the felons. Except, of course, that one police story fits that of the felons too. Alone of the policemen on the roof, Claude Pain *had* heard Bentley talk before that night. He had met him before on street corners and the boy had spoken to him. There was no mention of the phrase 'Let him have it,' in Pain's deposition. 'I did not write it down because I did not hear it. I did not write it down because it was not said.'

The phrase itself of course is the kind of gangster idiom which *might* have come from Bentley, though much more probably from Craig. But in fact, John Parris reveals where it came from:

> Nobody has yet [1960] however called attention to the striking similarities between this case and the facts and the words used in Rex v. Appleby (1940), 28 Criminal Appeal Reports. Appleby and another man were engaged in a warehouse-breaking venture when they were interrupted by a police officer. The other man shot that officer. In his dying declaration, the officer said that Appleby had incited the other to fire by using the words 'Let him have it, he is all alone.'
>
> 'Let him have it . . .' They were the words that hanged Appleby.
> 'Let him have it . . .' They were the words that hanged Bentley.
>
> It is a strange coincidence that, in the only two reported cases this century of joint liability for the murder of a police officer, exactly the same words should have been used. The case of Appleby is, of course, one that anybody would look up if they wanted to know whether, if one of two housebreakers does the shooting, the other one can be found guilty of murder.
>
> But this is largely immaterial.

It was only 'largely immaterial' to Parris in 1960 because he had no idea of the presence, let alone the conflicting testimony, of Claude Pain. It is now, in the light of both, highly material.

Frank Cassels hinted perhaps at collusion in his cross-examination of Fairfax:

'Officer, when did you make notes, as I imagine you did, of what was said on the roof-top?'

'I did not make any notes,' said Fairfax.

'No notes at all?'

'No; I dictated a statement.'

'When did you dictate the statement?'

'It was after receiving medical attention at the hospital; somewhere between one and two in the morning of the 3rd November.'

'Had a number of other police officers been to see you in hospital before you dictated the statement?'

'No.'

'None at all?'

'I saw Detective Chief Inspector Smith and Detective Sergeant Shepherd at the hospital when they came in.'*

The same Detective Chief Inspector Smith who, Iris Bentley told me, had kicked Derek in the face by the time his family first saw him in Brixton Prison. His father asked him how his face had come to be bruised and puffy. A patrolling prison warder interrupted to disallow the question. But Derek was able to tell his family later that Smith had told him to take out his shoelaces on his arrival at Croydon Police Station. As he bent over, Smith drove his boot against Derek's head. It is almost certain that a blow like that caused a fit. And another police officer of Z Division, who prefers not be named, remembers being shocked by the boy's injuries.

What I believe happened is this. All the police officers on the roof, indeed the hundred or more finally called to the scene, were naturally outraged at the death of Sidney Miles, a good copper, honest and brave, who had only three years to go to his retirement. But when it was realized that Craig was only sixteen and Bentley innocent of Miles's murder then something had to be done. Did someone remember 'Let him have it' from the Appleby case? Had someone read it in the books available in the Fell Road police station? It had already hanged Appleby. It could now hang Bentley. The magistrate's hearing at Croydon court the next day made no mention of the phrase. It lasted only six minutes, was conducted in haste, and the only police witness called was DCI Smith, who had seen Fairfax in hospital and who in any case gave no hard evidence at that stage at all.

It was of course a risk that conflicting testimony, i.e. Pain's, might be heard at the magistrates' court, but it was a calculated one. David Lewis and Peter Hughman in *Just How Just?* make the point that the magistrates' courts are dominated by the police to such an extent that they are often referred to as police courts. 'Moreover,' they write, 'this power [to arrest, charge and bring prosecution] is often vested in

---

* *Notable British Trials* op. cit.

junior officers who may be subject to considerable pressures but very little supervision.'

In my view, the trial of Craig and Bentley was convened with indecent haste – only five weeks after the event and only *two days* after Parris, defending Craig, received his brief. A solicitor of my acquaintance has told me that nowadays the usual time taken for a case of this nature to come to trial is between twelve and eighteen *months*. For whatever reason, McDonald was not prepared to swear that Bentley had said the damning phrase. Harrison was. Presumably the 'facts' were duly entered in these men's depositions, either at a first or second draft. They were certainly there by 17 November when the depositions were presented for the Prosecution brief.

A report in *Justice* (organ of the British Branch of the International Commission of Jurists) looking into the prosecution process in England and Wales in 1970 said:

> The honest, zealous and conscientious police officer who has satisfied himself that the suspect is guilty, becomes psychologically committed to prosecution and thus to successful prosecution. He wants to prosecute and he wants to win.

– perhaps at any cost. Perhaps at the cost of a human life. The life of Derek Bentley.

Again, Lewis and Hughman:

> Whilst we accept that the police have no official mandate for delinquent behaviour, we would argue that the existing system gives them enormous opportunities for the misapplication of power . . . Furthermore, police officers investigate criminal offences without effective supervision . . . as they are frequently the most important prosecution witnesses they often provide the most probative evidence. It is all too easy for them to misrepresent what a defendant has said or invent admissions . . . In cases where they are convinced of a defendant's guilt, but feel the evidence they can present is not enough to make conviction a certainty, the temptation to act in this manner must be considerable . . . a corrupt officer has power to punish by fabricating evidence.

Lewis and Hughman cite the examples of DS Harry Challenor in June 1964, beatings of suspects by the police in Sheffield in 1963 and widespread allegations into misconduct in the Met in 1973, leading to the creation of the A10 internal investigation department. Apropos of the Challenor case, Arthur James QC said:

> In a disciplined force there is always the temptation to disregard a rule, to take a short cut or to subscribe to the view that the end justifies the means of getting there. An atmosphere can grow which undermines discipline and produces wrongful acts. It is an atmosphere in which the lower ranks know they are allowed to do those things provided they are not found out and that no one is going to try very hard to find out.*

A Royal Commission in 1962 reported that 32% of the public believed that the police distorted evidence in court. Public opinion is hardly fact, but the sense of alienation among the police themselves which this sort of finding illustrates, '. . . combined with a belief that the general public neither appreciates nor cares about the difficulties of their work, could explain why some officers are prepared to break the law in order to enforce it, whilst many more will give tacit support to such behaviour by their silence.'**

Lewis and Hughman also note that when the police are under-strength (as the Met habitually is); when they are therefore working long hours (look again at DS Shepherd's duty on the night in question); when there is a rising crime rate (as there had been in South London's violent playground) this tendency is likely to be exacerbated –

> . . . particularly when the police are dealing with an enormous caseload against a background of rising crime and public agitation, it is hardly surprising that some officers are prepared to use extreme means to obtain results. It is equally unremarkable that breaches of discipline will be condoned by colleagues and senior officers.***

Of the Sheffield beatings, Lewis and Hughman write:

> One senior officer had concocted an account of what took place and the detectives were told to give this false evidence in court. Not one man on the force who knew of the incidents had reported them.

* *Just How Just* by David Lewis and Peter Hughman, London 1975
** Ibid
*** Ibid

Indeed, all the research evidence suggests it would have been remarkable had they done so . . .

It is not likely then, if this book is ever read by present or past members of Z Division, or indeed any policemen anywhere, that such readers will be glad that a case of appalling injustice has been uncovered. Rather they will dismiss it as another anti-police book, another product of the soft, anti-authoritarianism of this end of our century. During my researches for this book I rang Mr Bill Waddell, ex-policeman and currently curator of Scotland Yard's Black Museum. He kindly consented to see me at short notice on a miserable, wet day in the middle of February. The taxi took me past Norman Shaw's Opera House – the 'real' Scotland Yard of the Craig and Bentley period – on to the ghastly glass and chrome monolith outside which the triangular sign always turns. In the entrance way, full of very tall people in and out of uniform, an eternal flame burns to commemorate those who died during the war. The Roll of Honour book was open on that 13th of February at the page recording the death by gunshot of PC Nathaniel Edgar.

There were passes to be filled in and strict security was observed. I felt like an intruder. This was a private place where everyone talked in hushed tones. It was like a church. And I was not of the faith. Waddell took me up to his office on the umpteenth floor. His tone was hectoring and he lectured me for over ten minutes on his contempt for writers who invent unsupportable theories. He had a file of papers on his desk to which I had already formally been denied access. To be fair to him, he offered me access to them, but the offer was half-hearted. He was a busy man, in a hurry.

He flicked the catch on a side door, which reminded me of Wandsworth with its adjacent execution shed, and we crept into the Holy of Holies, the Museum itself where a party of ghoulish tourists was being shown the rows of death masks and the implements of torture. The knuckleduster which Craig had made, which Bentley had carried, which Goddard had used, did look quite nasty. But in the martial-arts-dominated 1980's, it is relatively tame and the 'spike' is nothing of the sort, merely a blunt projection. The sawn-off Eley, with the rest of its barrel alongside, looked bigger than I had imagined. I let the cold, twisted brass of a spent bullet lie in my hand for a moment. Bentley's knife was there, and Craig's, and an assortment of other items which I was not allowed to dwell on.

Mr Waddell wanted to know what my angle was. He was plainly suspicious of me and, I felt, of outsiders generally. He approved of Goddard. He approved of hanging. His view of British justice was distorted to the extent that he believed it was up to Parris and Cassels to prove Craig and Bentley innocent rather than for Humphreys and Bass to prove them guilty.

'There's been a lot of shit written about this case,' he said. 'And most of it has come our way.'

This, I suspect, will be the attitude of the Metropolitan Police. I hope I am wrong. But if I am not, it is no more than many people have come to expect.

But there was in 1952 one unfortunate problem. The deposition of PC Pain made no mention of the phrase, 'Let him have it, Chris.' Rather than risk a conflict of police testimony in open court, with all the delicious opportunities this would present to the defence, Pain's deposition disappeared. So too must his presence on the rooftop. So the other policemen on the roof avoided that presence. Fairfax, McDonald, Harrison and Jaggs were all feet and sometimes inches away from him, yet not one of them mentions him at all. The only oblique reference to Pain is the ubiquitous 'other officers' travelling in the police van. It was Derek Bentley's bad luck that PC Pain was not after all required to testify at the magistrate's court. And his non-appearance at the Old Bailey was fatally unfortunate. Claude Pain was a copper of the old school. He wouldn't let his mates down. Mike Seabrook sums it up in talking about idle coppers, but surely it applies more so in the case of overtly honest ones –

[Such men] . . . 'had committed the unforgiveable sin; they let their mates down, and they were not forgiven . . . officers such as these *do* walk in fear; for they know what their comrades know.'

And Sidney Miles was a mate. Pain would not want his death to go unpunished any more than Fairfax or Harrison or McDonald or Jaggs. Besides, Pain had less than two years to go for a pension; and he had a wife and three kids . . .

'Some very funny things were going on in those days, Mr Trow,' Pain told me, 'I could be hit by a car or anything.'

There is of course one simple way in which the veracity of Pain's statement – and those of Bentley and Craig in this respect – can be put to the test. We can ask the participants. I was unable to locate Christopher Craig. According to one source he has changed his name and gone to ground, marrying and applying to emigrate to New Zealand, which turned him down. He gave interviews to Victor Gollancz the publisher on his release from prison and to David Yallop in 1971. Since then he has retired from the field. Because of the interest in the case generated by Elvis Costello's 'Let him Dangle', *The People* newspaper tracked Craig down and he appears, fat, bearded and bald, in an article printed by them on June 4th 1989. He is a plumber, married with two children and lives in a village in Bedfordshire. I wrote to him and he declined to answer. Since the article, the plumber has gone ex-directory! But I see no reason why his version of events should have altered since the trial. He did not hear Bentley or anybody else say 'Let him have it, Chris'. Derek Bentley is dead. So is Robert Jaggs; so is James McDonald. Of the policemen on the roof, only Pain, Harrison and Fairfax are left. I have written to Fairfax and Harrison and have received replies, one direct, the other indirect, from both. Fairfax's letter to me, dated 8 December 1988, simply reads:

Thank you for your letter dated 6th inst. I wish to inform you that I am neither prepared to meet you or to discuss the case with you.

Harrison's is altogether more interesting. He has in fact replied to the Press Office at Scotland Yard, who were kindly helping with my research. April Goodey of that office wrote to me on 17 December:

I received a reply to your request from a former PC Norman Harrison who declines to participate in any way with your book.

He has also asked me to pass on a warning to you that he is prepared to sue if the publication contains any inaccuracies 'factual or otherwise'.

I am sorry to pass a message of this kind to you in these circumstances and can assure you it was most unexpected, as obviously an officer in the case could help where accuracy is concerned . . .

The reader who has stayed with me thus far will be less surprised than was Ms Goodey at Harrison's attitude. He had a chance in 1970 and

1971; he has a chance now, to set the record straight, to clarify the roof-top 'gun battle'. I gave no hint in my letter to Harrison or to the Yard's Press Office of the direction in which my researches were taking me. What therefore has Harrison to hide? And if he remains silent, what right does he have to sue over 'inaccuracies factual or otherwise'? Harrison, like Jaggs and McDonald, did not agree to an interview with Yallop in 1971; there is no reason for him to change his mind now. I am convinced that experts like Haler, the pathologist, and Nickolls, the ballistics officer, can help no further. Their entire findings were presented, however disappointingly, at the trial. John Parris and Frank Cassels were working in the dark in that they did not have all the material evidence and testimony at their disposal. I do not know at this distance of time whether even the prosecution had the testimony of PC Pain. Humphreys is dead and J. S. Bass died long ago.

I turned therefore to my second obvious line of enquiry – the Metropolitan Police themselves. I wrote to Croydon Police Station – now long removed, of course, from Fell Road with its 'dungeons' and its underground passage to the magistrates' court – and received no reply at all. The Yard were altogether more helpful. I was perfectly at liberty to visit the famous Black Museum, but all records relating to the Craig and Bentley case were housed at the Public Record Office at Kew in the File marked MEPO 2/9401. Curious then that Bill Waddell should have a file of papers in his office. The Yard's Departmental Records Officer told me that the Kew files were not available to the public for seventy-five years and I could not therefore see them until the year 2047. Since I shall then be 98 years old, I really did not relish the wait!

I tried the Directory of Public Prosecutions (now the Crown Prosecution Service) asking to borrow – as David Yallop had apparently done – the transcript of the trial. I was told that this was only done in the most unusual circumstances and the CPS's Departmental Records Officer had no knowledge of the circumstances by which it was lent to Yallop. He believed the copy available in the Notable British Trials series was probably edited and wanted to know more details about me and why I wished to see the original transcript. To date, I have received no reply to my second letter giving this information.

It occurred to me that one possible way to find the original police depositions was to apply to Croydon Magistrates' Court in the hope that something from Z Division would be lodged there. In reply to my letter the Clerk to the Justices told me that all depositions taken in the committal for trial proceedings would have been forwarded to the Central Criminal Court (Old Bailey), as Croydon were only obliged to keep them for three years after November 1952. I have received no reply to my subsequent letter along these lines to the Old Bailey.

In desperation I tried a compromise. I wrote to Kew asking whether, among the relevant papers, there were the depositions of Pain, Beecher-Brigden and Alderson, Yallop's 'three monkeys' who 'vanished into the ranks of policemen'. This query could not be answered by Kew and the buck was passed back to the Yard, whose Assistant Departmental Records Officer (was I now being shunted down the line?) told me curtly: 'I regret to say we are unable to disclose any information from a closed file.'

It took a visit to Iris Bentley for me to see *some* of the Home Office files. She has campaigned for years to be allowed to see the relevant papers. A parcel of these was in fact sent to her. They contain a portion only of the Prosecution brief – depositions of Haler, the pathologist; of the policemen DCI Smith, DS Shepherd, DS Fairfax and Constables Harrison and McDonald; a list of trial witnesses; a list of Prosecution exhibits; formal notification of the dismissed Appeal; medical and psychiatric reports on Craig and Bentley which Christopher Berry-Dee is so excited about; and a rather pointless deposition from an eighteen-year-old postal clerk called Jean Brimblecombe dated 1 December which was not used at the trial and seems to have no bearing on the case at all.

Iris Bentley's most recent request to the Home Office to see all the files was turned down in 1987 because of the 'sensitive material' they contained. My own request to them along similar lines elicited a curious circular argument in reply. The Public Records Act of 1958 and 1967 lays down what is and is not available to the public (a curious choice of title then – *Public* Records). In capital cases like that of Derek Bentley, closure is for seventy-five years. The sinister-sounding 'sensitive material' is merely Home Office jargon for 'closed to the public'. In other words, we are no further forward. In other words it is time that the Home Office, indeed Government departments generally, took a fairer position over such files. If a case is closed (as that of Craig and Bentley is) then what can be the harm in making its entire contents open to the public? To do otherwise could imply that there is some pressing need for such files to remain dormant. Can the British judicial system really be so frail that it cannot rattle its skeletons in the open and not in some cupboard at Kew?

I contacted the Yard's Press Office at least hoping to learn what I could about the men of Z Division and their careers prior to the roof-top incident. In being passed on the phone from department to department from the famous switchboard number of 230 1212, I actually heard a young man while presumably cupping his mouthpiece in a careless manner say, 'There's some bloke here wanting to know about old crimes. That's peculiar, isn't it?'

And even when I got to the Press Office I had to explain as though to an alien space crew who Craig and Bentley were and in a nutshell what happened on that Croydon night thirty-seven years ago . . .

Even the BBC let me down. The documentary drama hailed by them in 1972 as the 'scoop of the year' and shown again in 1973, remembered vividly by Mrs Beecher-Brigden whose husband rang up to complain about its inaccuracies, has vanished without trace. The BBC could only suggest that I should contact the programme's author, who 'may be able to help you further.' Curiouser and curiouser . . .

I don't believe I should have to wait until 2047. In the interests of justice, the police files on Craig and Bentley should be available to me – to any member of the public – now. Then we would know how many guns were issued to the police, precisely to whom, and whether any rounds were fired by them. Then we could read for ourselves the original statements made by men hours after the event. I see no logical reason why the depositions of Allan Beecher-Brigden and James Alderson should not be among them. After all, neither of them was on the roof. There can be little doubt that Bentley's argument – that he did not know Craig had a gun – was a spurious one, a lie. So Alderson's testimony is unlikely to have rattled that presumption even if it did differ from that of Roberts and Stephens, the other officers in the car taking Bentley to the station. And I cannot imagine what in Beecher-Brigden's statement did not accord with the orthodox version from the roof. Yet I know that Pain and Beecher-Brigden at least did make depositions. Pain wrote his in longhand copied from the notes in his notebook.

And I am afraid I am cynical enough to believe that when they do open the police files on Craig and Bentley, there will be no deposition from Claude Pain. That will have gone to the 1952 version of the shredder a long time ago – as will his pocketbook, the one he had to hand in to the station when it was full. Like his helmet and his truncheon, it was the property of the Metropolitan Police.

Since the day the trial of Craig and Bentley ended on Thursday, 11 December 1952, the world has known that a miscarriage of justice took place. That knowledge was based on an ambiguous law interpreted by a biased judge who had decided the guilt of the defendants before his backside touched the Bench. And the knowledge made no difference to the crowd who howled for the blood of a cosh boy. Or to the Home Secretary who, despite the jury's recommendation for mercy, gave that crowd precisely what they wanted.

With the publication of this book has come the knowledge, I hope, that there was a double miscarriage in the case of Craig and Bentley. I am a law-abiding citizen myself in the conventional sense of the term. Like every other property owner and professional person approaching middle age, I would probably have howled for Bentley's blood too. Until, that is, I realized that he was, in the parlance of the underworld, 'stitched up'. Even now it is difficult to make some people open their eyes. One publisher who turned down this book found the 'fifth policeman theory *interesting*'. It is not a theory. It is hard, concrete evidence and if it had been produced at the Old Bailey might well have been enough to save Derek Bentley from the gallows.

Goddard ironically posed the question himself during his summing up:

> There is one thing I am sure I can say with the assent of all you twelve gentlemen, that the police officers that night, and those three officers in particular [Fairfax, McDonald and Harrison] showed the highest gallantry and resolution; they were conspicuously brave. Are you going to say they are conspicuous liars?

The jury said no. Theirs was the only evidence on which Derek Bentley could be hanged. And he *was* hanged to encourage the others; to deter other would-be delinquents of his day and to reassure the police forces of this country that their efforts were not in vain.

> Rightly or wrongly, [wrote C. G. L. Du Cann in 1960] in modern England the lives and safety of policemen tend to be regarded as more important than those of other citizens . . . The case of Bentley certainly suffered from the 'official' atmosphere prevailing at the time. The country was short of police; an epidemic of serious violence afflicted the country; the prevalence of juvenile crime was worrying the authorities. Again, the homicidal teenager was re-

garded as a social phenomenon which needed deterrence. Perhaps, too, the fact that Craig could not be hanged made the authorities more determined to hang Bentley . . .

Apologists for Goddard, apologists for counsel, prosecution and defence, in the case, claim that all acted as they did because recent experience had suggested that Bentley – particularly with the jury's recommendation to mercy – would be reprieved. Goddard himself was said to have been surprised that Maxwell-Fyfe was not more lenient. Perhaps the police view was rather different. This time, perhaps, reprieve would not come.

Most people reading this book will ask the same question that has been put to me countless times since I began writing. Why didn't Pain come forward at the time? Why hasn't he come forward since? At the time I believe he thought that other officers knew more than he did. It was not his decision not to appear in court, but that of his superiors – presumably the CID officer whose case it was, DCI John Smith. When he was not called either at Croydon or the Bailey, Pain asked why. The CID answered with a shrug. A shrug that said, although Pain did not know it, 'Your evidence doesn't fit the pattern, old son. Keep your head down and it'll be all right.' He had a wife and three children. His pension was less than two years away. We don't have to cite the American policeman 'Serpico' to know the opprobrium dished out to officers who turn against their brothers. There are examples of it in British forces. It is an utterly thankless task and a desolately lonely road. It was not until the mid-seventies that Pain read Yallop's book and not until 1988 that he chose to unburden himself to me. Only then did he see for the first time the damning evidence of his colleagues; their full testimony at the trial.

Claude Pain is an honourable man. The recipient of citations for valour and good conduct, he should have been given a medal for his part in the gun-fight on the roof. That he was not and that he has never complained about it is testimony enough to the kind of man he is. When I sent him photocopies of the trial evidence of Fairfax, Mc-Donald, Harrison and Jaggs, he quietly wrote his own version in the margins, but has never once called any one of them a liar, conspicuous or otherwise. How long he agonized over whether to tell someone what he knows, only he can tell. But Claude Pain is an old man.

Perhaps he feels it is time to get all this off his chest. If so, then this book is for him.

When I began writing this book, I confess it was with a novelist's instinct for a good story. As I progressed, the book became a quiet crusade. I hope that when this book hits the bookstores, something will also hit the fan. It is not enough for the Craig and Bentley case to remain a judicial curiosity gathering dust on library shelves, a talking point for rising generations of barristers over their port. It is not enough for smug publishers to offer patronizing comments on the interest of the 'fifth policeman theory'. It is not enough for successive Home Secretaries from David Maxwell-Fyfe to Douglas Hurd to shrug and mutter about 'sensitive issues'. The whole fabric of society depends on justice not only being done, but being seen to be done. Claude Pain deserves a medal for his actions on that Croydon rooftop.

And more importantly, Derek Bentley deserves a pardon for his.

In the last letter to his family which Bentley dictated to a prison officer at Wandsworth the day before he died, he said:

> 'Oh Dad! Don't let my cycle frames get rusty they might come in handy one day 'cos old Sally has got a cracked frame and I want you to change it before something happens to you, and Dad, keep a strict eye on Denis if he does anything wrong, though I don't think he will but you never know how little things can get you into trouble, if he does, wallop him so that he won't be able to sit for three weeks. I am trying to give you good advice because of my experience.
>
> I tell you what Mum, the truth of this story has got to come out one day, and as I said in the visiting box that one day a lot of people are going to get into trouble and I think you know who those people are . . .*

This book is for him, too.

* 'My Son's Execution' Bentley op. cit.

BENTLEY AND CRAIG

Ralph McTell

In 1952 in Croydon
There was bomb sites still around from the war
November that year food was scarcely off the ration
Two boys went out to rob a store.

Craig he was just about sixteen years old
Bentley he was nineteen
But Craig had a shooter stuck in his pocket
Made him feel more like a man.

Out on the roof of Barlow and Parker
Somebody saw them there
In a matter of minutes the police had arrived
And when they saw them you can bet those boys were scared.

Craig he shouted that he had a gun
And he thought about the movies that he'd seen
Back at Fell Road they signed the rifles out
And arrived very quick back on the scene.

Some of the police got onto the roof
Bentley knew that he could not escape
So he gave himself up and they put him under arrest
And he begged his young friend Chris won't you do the same.

Give me the gun the sergeant cried
Let him have it Chris poor Bentley said
But a shot rang out well it tore the night in half
Well the poor policeman was lying there dead.

Some people said it was a bullet from Craig's gun
That laid that policeman away
Some people said it was a police marksman's bullet
Some people said it could be a ricochet.

Both was found guilty of murder Craig he was too young not yet a man
Though he was under arrest when the fatal shot was fired
Derek Bentley was judged old enough to hang
Bentley he was judged to be a man.

Twenty three of January in Wandsworth Prison
When they took poor Bentley's life
Some people shouted and some people prayed
Some people just hung their heads and cried.

Oh you men on our behalf who sanctioned that boy's death
There's still one thing left to do
You can pardon Derek Bentley who never took a life
For Derek Bentley cannot pardon you

Derek Bentley cannot pardon you.

© Misty River Music 1982.

LET HIM DANGLE

Elvis Costello

Bentley said to Craig 'Let him have it, Chris'
They still don't know today just what he meant by this
Craig fired the pistol, but was too young to swing
So the police took Bentley and the very next thing
Let him dangle
Let him dangle.

Bentley had surrendered, he was under arrest,
When he gave Chris Craig that fatal request
Craig shot Sidney Miles, he took Bentley's word
The prosecution claimed as they charged them
With murder
Let him dangle
Let him dangle.

They say Derek Bentley was easily led
Well, what's that to the woman that Sidney Miles wed
Though guilty was the verdict and Craig had shot him dead
The gallows were for Bentley and still she never said
Let him dangle
Let him dangle.

Well it's hard to imagine its the times that have changed
When there's a murder in the kitchen that is brutal and strange
If killing anybody is a terrible crime
Why does this bloodthirsty chorus come round from time to time
Let him dangle

Not many people thought that Bentley would hang
But the word never came, the phone never rang
Outside Wandsworth Prison there was horror and hate
As the hangman shook Bentley's hand to calculate his weight
Let him dangle

From a Welfare State to society murder
'Bring back the noose' is always heard
Whenever those swine are under attack
But it won't make you even
It won't bring him back
Let him dangle
Let him dangle (string him up).

BIBLIOGRAPHY

ASCOLI, DAVID: *The Queen's Peace – The Origins and Development of the Metropolitan Police 1829–1979*, Hamish Hamilton 1979.

BENTLEY, W. G.: *My Son's Execution*, W. H. Allen 1957.

BERRY-DEE, CHRISTOPHER and ODELL, ROBIN: *Dad Help Me Please*, W. H. Allen 1990.

BLAND, JAMES: *True Crime Diary Vols 1 and 2*, Futura 1986.

BRESLER, FENTON: *Lord Goddard*, Harrap 1977.

COHEN, ALBERT K: *Delinquent Boys*, 1956.

DU CANN, C. G. L: *Miscarriages of Justice*, Frederick Muller 1960.

DUFF, CHARLES: *A Handbook on Hanging*, E. P. Publishing 1974.

ELSWORTH, STEVE: *Acid Rain*, Pluto 1984.

FURNEAUX, RUPERT: *They Died by a Gun*, Herbert Jenkins 1962.

GAUTE, J. H. H. and ODELL, ROBIN: *Murder 'Whatdunit'?*, Harrap 1982.

GAUTE, J. H. H. and ODELL, ROBIN: *The Murderers' Who's Who*, Harrap 1979.

JACKSON, STANLEY: *The Old Bailey*, W. H. Allen 1978.

KENNEDY, LUDOVIC: *On My Way to the Club*, Collins 1989.

LEWIS, DAVID and HUGHMAN, PETER: *Just How Just?* Secker and Warburg 1975.

LOCK, JOAN: *Blue Murder? Policemen under Suspicion*, Robert Hale 1986.

MARK, ROBERT: *In The Office of Constable*, Collins, 1978.

MAYS, JOHN BARRON: *Crime and the Social Structure*, Faber and Faber 1963.

MONTGOMERY HYDE, H.: *The Trial of Craig and Bentley* (Notable British Trials Series); William Hodge and Co. 1954.

MORRIS, TERENCE: *The Criminal Area*, 1957.

PAGET, R. T. and SILVERMAN, S. S.: *Hanged – and Innocent?*, Victor Gollancz 1953.

PALMER, TONY: *All You Need is Love: The Story of Popular Music*, Weidenfeld and Nicolson, 1976.

PARRIS, E. JOHN: *Most of my Murders*, Frederick Miller 1960.

PIERREPOINT, ALBERT: *Executioner: Pierrepoint*, Harrap 1974.

Science against Crime: Marshall Cavendish 1982.

SEABROOK, MIKE: *Coppers – An Inside View of the British Police*, Harrap 1987.

SELWYN, FRANCIS: *Gangland – The Case of Bentley and Craig*, Routledge 1988.

SYMONS, JULIAN: *Bloody Murder*, Penguin 1972.

WERTHAM, FREDRIC: *The Seduction of the Innocent*, Museum Press 1954.

YALLOP, DAVID A: *To Encourage the Others*, W. H. Allen, 1971.

NEWSPAPERS AND PERIODICALS:

Daily Mail
Sunday Pictorial
Croydon Advertiser
Croydon Times
Daily Telegraph
Daily Express
Croydon Post
Picture Post
Police Review

INDEX